Supervising
Music in the
Elementary School

PRENTICE-HALL INTERNATIONAL, INC., *London*
PRENTICE-HALL OF AUSTRALIA, PTY., LTD., *Sydney*
PRENTICE-HALL OF CANADA, LTD., *Toronto*
PRENTICE-HALL OF INDIA (PRIVATE) LTD., *New Delhi*
PRENTICE-HALL OF JAPAN, INC., *Tokyo*

Supervising
Music in the
Elementary School

EDWARD J. HERMANN

School of Music
Louisiana State University

PRENTICE-HALL, INC., ENGLEWOOD CLIFFS, NEW JERSEY

TO

Lillian, Carol, Susan and Jim

Preface

There is a considerable body of professional literature dealing with methods and materials in elementary music education. However, there is little that deals directly with supervisory problems in the field. It is to the supervision of music in the elementary program that this book is addressed.

This book is concerned primarily with the elementary music specialist and her role in the elementary school. It is intended to assist the practicing specialist as well as to give the prospective specialist some concept of the nature of the task. However, the cooperative approach to elementary music education also calls for the interest and participation of others, particularly, the elementary teacher and the elementary principal. The supervisor of music, the general supervisor of instruction, and certain members of the central office staff are directly involved. It is hoped that this book will also be helpful to other curriculum workers who have a responsibility for instruction or supervision of the elementary music program.

Although various current approaches found in actual practice are examined in some detail, the reader will soon discover that the writer is of the opinion that the cooperative approach involving the elementary teacher, the music consultant, and the principal offers the most promise for developing an effective, on-going program.

As in any undertaking of this nature, the writer is indebted to many people. He is particularly grateful to his co-authors of the *Growing with Music* series: Dr. Harry Wilson, Chairman of the Music Department of Teachers College, Columbia University; Dr. Alice M. Snyder, Associate Professor of Music Education, San Francisco State College; Mr. Walter Ehret, Supervisor of Vocal Music, Scarsdale, New York Public Schools; and Dr. Albert A. Renna, Director of Music, San Francisco Unified School

District. They were most influential in shaping the writer's point of view concerning the teaching of music as an aesthetic discipline. Although not presuming to speak for them, he acknowledges their influence.

Dr. Robert Gilmore of the University of Southwestern Louisiana and Mr. Roy C. Welch, Superintendent of Schools in LaSalle Parish, Louisiana, worked closely with the writer in carrying out the research studies reported in the chapter "Current Practice." And to Dr. John Greene, Director of Instruction in the public schools of Baton Rouge, special acknowledgment is made for reacting to the material on child growth and development. Thanks are also extended to Mr. William Hartshorn of Los Angeles, Dr. George K. Evans of New York City, and Mrs. Lucile D'Aubin of Baton Rouge for critical readings of the manuscript. The writer also expresses his appreciation to his professional colleagues of the Caddo Parish Schools, the Louisiana State Department of Education, and Louisiana State University. Especial thanks to my wife for her encouragement and support in the preparation of this work.

EDWARD J. HERMANN

Contents

*Supervising
Music in the
Elementary School*

Part One

Music in the

Elementary School

1

Who Teaches Music
in the Elementary School?

The question, "Who is responsible for the teaching of music in the elementary school?" is a challenging and persisting one. The aim of elementary music education—to help children grow musically—has been quite clearly established. However, we are far from unanimous agreement as to the means for achieving this goal.

The elementary school merits the greatest possible attention and emphasis, for it is widely accepted that instruction in music at this level is the right of every child. Because of this fact, educators recognize that there is a tremendous potential in an effective elementary music program. Along with this potential, they identify some real and, at times, conflicting concerns.

Current Approaches

There is wide divergence in current practice regarding the teaching of music at the elementary level. This divergence may be exemplified by considering three hypothetical situations.

In the Northwest Township Schools one music specialist is assigned to each elementary building. All music teaching is done by this music teacher. The children of every grade come to a special music room three times a week. Some attempts are made to correlate music with other subjects but, for the most part, music is taught as a subject apart from the general program.

In the Plainfield County Schools, there are no elementary music specialists. The general instructional supervisor encourages the elementary teachers to make use of recordings and other teaching aids. Several, but not all, school faculties include one or two teachers who play the piano for school assemblies. Elementary teachers who have had some background in music attempt to assist others who have had little or no training.

In the Central City Schools, the school board employs five elementary music specialists as consultants who serve in fifteen elementary schools. Each music consultant works in three schools providing service to approximately thirty-five teachers. Elementary teachers, when employed, realize that they assume the responsibility for teaching music as they do any subject in the school program. Providing experiences in music for boys and girls is considered to be an endeavor involving the elementary teacher, the elementary principal, and the elementary music consultant.

Arguments have been made for each approach. With a music specialist doing most or all of the music teaching, one may assume that the teacher has the necessary background, interest, and ability to carry on an effective program. In Northwest Township, where the music specialist does all of the teaching, she[1] is well equipped to handle such problems as reading, listening, and part-singing. She knows a great deal about materials and resources. Her ability to play the piano and sing is an important asset in working with children. She has a depth of understanding in music far beyond the materials she uses in her teaching.

In the Plainfield County Schools, where there are no elementary music specialists, some elementary teachers are making an effort to provide music experiences in their classroom. If the teacher has a positive attitude toward music, if she has had adequate preparation in music, if she sees that music is an important experience for boys and girls, there are, indeed, advantages in her handling the music instruction. Music is used as it best fits into the schedule. Many opportunities are utilized to enrich and support other learnings.

However, it must also be admitted that there are many teachers in Plainfield County who have neither the skill nor the interest to teach music. In their classrooms music instruction is limited or is nonexistent.

---

[1] One of the encouraging trends in elementary music education is the increasing number of men who have become teacher-supervisors. However, by far the greater number of elementary music specialists are women. For this reason, the feminine pronoun is employed as a third person reference to the elementary music specialist throughout this book.

Definition of Terms

Up to this point we have used a number of descriptive titles that must be clearly defined before we may proceed further. In order to avoid confusion, these titles will be used consistently throughout this book:

A *music teacher* is the specialist who is directly responsible for teaching music to elementary children. If she works with classroom teachers, it is only in an incidental manner. She may teach in a special music room. If she teaches in the regular classrooms she will have opportunities to react with elementary teachers, but the teachers do not feel that teaching music is a part of their responsibility.

A *music consultant* also does direct teaching but her major mission is to work cooperatively with elementary teachers so that they become more and more independent of her help. The elementary teachers are expected to teach music. With some teachers the consultant may have to do a great deal of teaching. With other teachers who are quite independent musically, she may be able to restrict herself to the role of supervisor. The consultant usually works on a scheduled basis. Consultants working only "on call" or by request are rarely found in current practice.

The primary distinction between the music teacher and the music consultant is in the emphasis given to a cooperative role in working with teachers. The key point is whether elementary teachers are or are not expected to teach music as a part of their regular classroom responsibility.

The title *music specialist* as used in this book is an inclusive term applying to either a music teacher or a music consultant.

Perhaps these titles may be further clarified by these examples:

1. In referring to the person in the Northwest Township Schools who teaches children in a special music room, we are talking about a *music teacher*. The elementary teachers are not expected to teach music.

2. In referring to the person in the Central City Schools who works cooperatively with teachers in classroom visits and in in-service groups, we are talking about a *music consultant*. The elementary teachers are expected to teach music.

3. In recommending that the supervisor of music in a school system should meet regularly with his elementary *music specialists* we are saying that this is desirable practice whether the specialists happen to be music teachers or music consultants.

Between the two extremes of the music teacher who may spend all of her time in direct teaching and the music consultant who may spend all of her time in supervising there are many possible variations. This accounts for the proliferation of titles in current use: music teacher, music consultant, music specialist, elementary music supervisor, helping music teacher, vocal music teacher, public school music teacher, resource teacher, visiting music teacher, and itinerant teacher. For purposes of clarity we shall limit ourselves to three: (1) *music teacher,* (2) *music consultant,* and (3) the inclusive term, *music specialist.*

A *supervisor of music* is the person primarily responsible for the improvement of instruction in music. He has full supervisory and administrative responsibility for the total program of music education in a school system. Here we also find other titles. Director and coordinator are commonly used. To compound the confusion, he is also referred to as a consultant or as a specialist or as a resource person. Titles are determined for the most part by the staff organization of a particular school system. We shall refer consistently to the *supervisor of music.*

The Cooperative Approach

From the several possible approaches in elementary music education there is one which holds great promise as far as this writer is concerned. It is the approach in which the teaching of music in the elementary school is considered as a *cooperative* venture involving the elementary teacher, the music consultant, and the elementary principal. Others are also involved, but these are the key persons.

As is true of so many choices in education, the question of who is to teach music in the elementary school is not an either-or proposition. The cause of music education can best be served when the combined and cooperative efforts of teacher, consultant, and principal are brought into play. The cooperative approach offers the greatest possibility for the development of a vital, continuous program of music education in the elementary school.

The cooperative approach is a promising practice because it is productive. At its best, it combines the resources of the classroom teacher who is a specialist in knowing how children behave and learn at a particular stage of development and the music consultant who is highly skilled in a particular area of the curriculum. The combined efforts of both plus the coordination provided by the principal are necessary if a truly effective program of elementary music is to be developed.

No elementary music specialist, regardless of her ability, is able to plan and carry out a program of music for the elementary school entirely on her own initiative. The specialist may bring to the job good training, fine musicianship, and a genuine interest in boys and girls. However, she cannot possibly be aware of many of the possibilities for using music with a particular class during the limited time she is in the room. Even in Northwest Township where specialists do all of the music teaching, the music teacher must know what is going on in the general program to coordinate her music offerings effectively.

Miss Carol Jones, an elementary music consultant in the Central City Schools where music instruction is approached on a cooperative basis, visits Mrs. Susan Crandall's fourth-grade class for thirty minutes each week. Miss Jones knows the music activities that are appropriate for the fourth grade and it is to be expected that she will provide for them in her planning. However, it must also be recognized that Mrs. Crandall knows fourth graders in general and her children in particular. There are many possibilities for correlation that Miss Jones will have little or no opportunity to discover during the course of her weekly visits.

Some responsibilities in elementary music are primarily those of the elementary teacher. For example, using music as a "change-of-pace" activity is Mrs. Crandall's responsibility. She has found that music can be a stimulating variant in the daily schedule when both minds and muscles need a "stretch." No matter how often Miss Jones is able to visit, this particular use of music in the classroom will always remain Mrs. Crandall's responsibility.

Some responsibilities belong primarily to the music consultant. Although Mrs. Crandall has a positive attitude toward the teaching of music in her room, she is reluctant to initiate any activity involving music reading. In this area she feels inadequate. If music reading is to be taught in her class, it must be done by the consultant. When a new problem in music reading is to be presented in Mrs. Crandall's room, Miss Carol Jones shifts from the role of consultant to teacher.

However, in providing listening experiences, Miss Jones is pleased that Mrs. Crandall is willing to accept a shared responsibility. If Miss Jones will help her select appropriate recordings and suggest ways in which the recordings may be used, Mrs. Crandall agrees to include listening experiences in her teaching.

The sharing of responsibilities between Mrs. Susan Crandall, the elementary teacher, and Miss Carol Jones, the elementary music consultant, might be diagrammed like this:

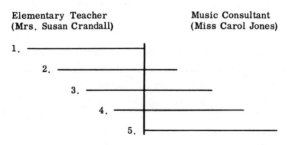

Elementary Teacher   Music Consultant
(Mrs. Susan Crandall)   (Miss Carol Jones)

In the above diagram, Line No. 1 might represent the "change-of-pace" use of music in the classroom. This Mrs. Crandall accepts as her responsibility. Line No. 3, equally divided between the teacher and consultant, might represent the listening phase of the program, where responsibility is jointly shared by teacher and consultant. Line No. 5 might represent the teaching of reading which, in this case, is the responsibility of the music consultant.

Line No. 2 might indicate an activity such as the use of simple instruments. Mrs. Crandall agrees that this is her responsibility primarily but she still requires some assistance from Miss Jones. Line No. 4 might represent the teaching of new songs which Miss Jones introduces. Mrs. Crandall is willing to rehearse these songs on the days that Miss Jones does not visit the class.

The five lines in the above diagram are, of course, arbitrary. The diagram indicates a cooperative responsibility for the music program that is jointly shared by the music consultant and the elementary teacher. To what extent the responsibilities are shared depends on the scope of the program, the musical ability of the elementary teacher, and the number of service visits the consultant is able to schedule.

It should be obvious that the above comments concerning shared responsibilities between Miss Jones and Mrs. Crandall will not be the same as the shared responsibilities between Miss Jones and Miss Mary Armstrong, or any other teacher. There will be variables for each teacher depending upon her background, interest, and ability. Miss Jones must be as sensitive to individual differences among elementary teachers as Mrs. Crandall is to differences among the children in her fourth-grade class.

The extent of shared responsibilities not only varies with each teacher but also depends on the personality and training of the music consultant. It should also be clear that the status of shared responsibilities does *not remain static.* As Miss Jones is able to work with a teacher over an extended period of time, the elementary teacher should be able to obtain more and more skills in music teaching that will make her less and less dependent on the help of the consultant. The long-range goal of every elementary music consultant should be to make it possible for each teacher whom she serves to discover herself musically and to become as musically independent as possible.

Although the diagram indicates the shared relationship between elementary teacher and consultant, it must be clearly understood that the cooperative approach cannot succeed without the close coordination and supervision of the principal. He not only is responsible for the program in action but also is equally responsible for its continued development. The success of the teacher-consultant relationship is largely due to the principal's efforts. In fact, it is more accurate to think of the cooperative approach as a *teacher-consultant-principal* relationship.

Impediments to the Cooperative Approach

One impediment to the cooperative approach is the attitude held by too many music educators that the great majority of elementary teachers are not interested in teaching music. It is true that many elementary teachers have strong reservations about their ability to teach music. In many cases they are literally frightened at the prospect of teaching some of its technical aspects. One of the challenging responsibilities of music supervision is to help the teacher find some phase of music in which she can make a successful beginning. Most elementary teachers would like to include music in their daily schedule.

A second impediment to the cooperative approach is that our musical expectations of elementary teachers have not always been realistic. Mursell highlights the problem when he says: "To ask that our teachers colleges equip all their prospective teachers with enough musical skill to function virtually as old-line supervisors, albeit on a low level of efficiency, is to seek the fantastically impossible."[2]

It is imperative that the music consultant set up expectations for classroom teachers on a realistic basis. Miss Carol Jones should challenge her teachers to grow musically over the years, but she must do so on the basis of each teacher's ability to cope with the challenge.

It is important that Miss Jones respect each teacher for what she can do musically. Nothing else gives the elementary teacher a greater sense of security. All elementary teachers are not proficient in all subjects. It is sometimes difficult for the consultant to realize that the teaching of music can be a formidable task to one who has had little or no training.

A third factor that negates the successful establishment of a cooperative relationship is the idea that the elementary music consultant, because of her involvement in music as a special interest, is quite insensitive to human behavior and to developmental principles. General educators sometimes assume that the music specialist knows very little about the broad concerns of education and even less about the behavior of boys and girls.

It is true that the visiting music consultant cannot come to know boys and girls as well as each classroom teacher. However, it is also true that in working with many boys and girls at all elementary grade levels, Miss Jones would be quite insensitive to behavior if she did not learn something about developmental patterns.

The Need for a Curriculum Policy Decision

One of the most pressing needs to assure the success of the elementary

[2] James L. Mursell, *Education for Musical Growth* (Boston: Ginn and Company, 1948), p. 305.

music program is the establishment of a clear-cut curriculum policy regarding the role the elementary music specialist is to play. Such a curriculum-
administrative policy decision facilitates the supervisory process as much as
any other single factor. For the elementary specialist it is important that she
understands whether she is to function primarily (1) as a *music consultant,*
that is, as one who does some direct teaching but whose primary role is to
work with elementary teachers to help them do a more effective job or (2)
as the *music teacher*—the person who does all or nearly all of the direct
teaching of music.

As has already been indicated, there is merit in each point of view. But
it is the height of frustration to a person like Carol Jones to accept a position
as an elementary music consultant only to discover that her principals and
the majority of teachers in the schools expect her to do all of the direct
teaching. A basic mode of operation needs to be established which all concerned understand and, if possible, in which all concerned concur.

Andrews and Cockerille have the following observation to make on
this point:

> Actually the main difficulty in getting the teamwork going between
> specialist and classroom teacher lies in a pathetic lack of interest in
> what is best for the pupils themselves.
> Who is to teach music should be a matter of *policy,* not happenstance.
> It should depend on the general supervisory policy of the school, who
> plans it, and how it is planned, and *who agrees to it.*[3]

This curriculum policy decision cannot be made only by music specialists. A definition of the role of the music specialist and the way in which she
is to work must be a decision involving all interested parties: the elementary
teacher, the music specialist, the principal, the general supervisor, and the
administrator. When this is done, the supervisory program can develop on
a sound basis.

Who Is Responsible for Music in the Elementary School?

No matter how skilled the music consultant, no matter how cooperative the principal, no matter how concerned the administrators, it is the
classroom teacher who will determine the day-by-day music instruction the
boys and girls in her classroom receive.

How the elementary teacher teaches music in her classroom depends
on a number of factors. The *attitude* of the elementary teacher is of great
importance. This attitude is determined by the sum total of experiences she
has had in music, in fact, by her lifetime contact with music. It is also more

[3] Frances M. Andrews and Clara E. Cockerille, *Your School Music Program*
(Englewood Cliffs, N. J.: Prentice-Hall, Inc., 1958), p. 36.

specifically influenced by her college preparation as well as in-service training on the job.

To be successful in music teaching, music must be of worth and significance to the teacher *as an individual*. Music must be important in her personal life. If music experiences have meaning to her as an individual, it follows that she will see music as having worth to her children in the classroom. A positive attitude toward music is indispensable.

Beyond attitude, it is necessary that the elementary teacher have some working skills. Although college-level preparation is important, it is surprising how often one overlooks other musical activities in the background of the elementary teacher in determining her ability to teach music. In Mrs. Crandall's case, the fact that she had piano lessons for six years is probably at least as important as the fact that she earned six semester hours in music education at State University.

The elementary music consultant can make important in-service contributions by providing enabling skills to individual teachers. Through direct help in the classroom, workshops, in-service study groups, the specialist can help a teacher who wants to do a better job of teaching music in many ways. The consultant must be able to recognize those things that the elementary teacher can do independently and encourage her to do them. She must identify those responsibilities which can be shared jointly if the teacher is given adequate help, encouragement, and guidance. And, finally, the consultant must recognize that in many classrooms some of the hoped-for learnings (such as music reading) can be achieved only if she does the actual teaching.

On the last point, some music consultants have guilt feelings in moving away from the "helping" teacher role to one of direct teaching. There is no reason for such concern. Many musical learnings, particularly at the upper elementary level, must be presented by one who has depth and experience in music.

The role of the principal, as we have already indicated, is vital. He is the supervisor of music in his school just as he is the supervisor of mathematics, language arts, and social studies. Perhaps his greatest contribution is in terms of *expectancy,* that is, in making clear to his faculty that experiences in music are as vital a part of the daily schedule as any other subject. In addition, he provides a real service in coordinating classroom visits of the music consultant so that her available time in his building is used to the best advantage.

If the school system has an overall supervisor of music, he can be influential in bringing about desired relationships, policies, and procedures that will result in an improvement of the elementary music education program. His presence in the central office and his peer status with other instructional supervisors help in promoting the acceptance of music as an integral part of the total program.

Summary

In this chapter we have pursued the basic question: who teaches music in the elementary schools? Although in some schools the music specialist does all of the music teaching while in others the elementary teacher has this sole responsibility, a cooperative approach involving teacher, consultant, and principal is the most practical as well as the most productive procedure.

The cooperative approach calls for responsibility being shared by teacher and consultant with supervision and coordination by the principal. The way in which responsibilities are shared depends upon a number of variables such as the schedule, the training of the elementary teacher, the personality of the consultant, and the scope of the music program.

The cooperative approach is dependent upon the positive support of the principal, reasonable expectations of the elementary teacher, and musical skill plus sensitivity to human behavior on the part of the consultant.

One of the greatest prerequisites for the success of a program of elementary music supervision is the establishment of a curriculum policy decision that sets forth very clearly the role of the elementary specialist. It should be a policy which all concerned understand and in which all concerned concur.

Questions for Discussion

1. Define the titles *music teacher, music consultant,* and *music specialist* as they are used in this chapter. What are some other titles that are used in current practice?

2. Discuss the *cooperative approach* to elementary music education. Who are the persons most directly involved?

3. In what ways is an elementary music specialist, even a very good one, limited in developing a comprehensive music program through her own efforts?

4. Why would the "shared responsibilities" between teacher and consultant not remain constant? Why would they probably not be the same for any two elementary teachers?

5. What is the principal's role in the cooperative approach?

6. What are some impediments or obstacles to the cooperative approach?

7. Is it possible for the specialist to decide for herself what her working role is to be? What is meant by the recommendation that the definition of her role should be a curriculum policy decision? Who is involved in making this decision?

8. Contrast the advantages and disadvantages of the *music teacher* approach with the *music consultant* approach. Which do you believe is the more common approach used in current practice?

9. Discuss the statement: "The elementary teacher is the key person in an elementary music program." True or untrue? Why?

10. Discuss the significance of the elementary teacher's *attitude* toward the teaching of music in the classroom.

2

The Role of Music in Elementary Education

Understanding the broad aims of education is as important for the music educator as for any educator. It is necessary that aims for music education in the elementary school be clearly established, but it is not until we have thought through the broad objectives of the total educational program that we can attempt to formulate aims for a particular area.

Aims, if they are to have any meaning, must be formulated in terms of people. Education, as we conceive it, has two major aims:

1. The development of the child into the best person he is capable of becoming.
2. The development of the child into a responsible, contributing member of our democratic society.

Perhaps one of the most widely accepted statements concerning the ultimate goal of education is the one in *The Central Purpose of American Education:* "The basic American value, respect for the individual, has led to one of the major charges which the American people have placed on their schools: to foster that development of individual capacities which will enable each human being to become the best person he is capable of becoming."[1]

[1] *The Central Purpose of American Education.* Educational Policies Commission, National Education Association, 1201 Sixteenth St., N.W., Washington, D. C., 1961, p. 1.

In simpler language we might say that the purpose of the school is to provide a long-time environment where children come together and where we help them become the kind of persons they hope to be within the setting of our American way of life. The worth and dignity of the individual and the possibility of limitless improvement of human experience are fundamental beliefs of a democratic society.

The public school is a great unifying force in our culture. It builds a unity based on human values such as the supreme worth and dignity of the individual. At the same time, it develops the realization that no conflict exists between the welfare of the individual and the best interests of the group which he serves.

What is the role of music education? Working from the basic aim of education, we may say that in music education we are concerned with how *music experiences* can contribute to the growth and development of the individual to the extent that he is able to contribute to the culture in which he lives. From the developmental point of view, the purpose of music teaching is to bring about, to foster, and to promote musical responsiveness or musicality.

On the point of musicality, Pitts has this admonition:

> Make no mistake about it, all children, all human beings are musical. Degrees of musical response differ, of course, since no two people ever have the same amount of anything. The mistake is to divide either children or grown-ups into the *haves* and *have-nots* as if special degrees of talent created special kinds of persons. It is nearer the truth *to regard the musician not as a special kind of person but every person as a special kind of musician.*[2]

Primary Concern for Aesthetic Values

Why should music be a core experience for children in the elementary school? An all-inclusive answer completely satisfactory to everyone associated with the elementary school has yet to be found. However, one basic premise fundamental to our viewpoint is that *aesthetic experience and growth are essentials of life.*

Aesthetic experiences are needed by all children everywhere, of any culture. Children are eager to explore new sights, new sounds, new colors, and new textures. This drive for sensory experience is universal although each culture seeks to satisfy these needs in different ways.

Music is not simply something that is "nice to have" in the elementary schools of our own culture. Our children *require* aesthetic satisfactions, including musical ones, as a part of their normal development. They *need* experiences in music not only for the sheer joy of its beauty but for the depth

[2] Lilla Belle Pitts, "The General Music Program in the Elementary School," *National Elementary Principal,* Volume XXX, Number 4 (February, 1951), p. 5.

of feeling and emotion it is able to communicate. Only by responding to music and by participating in making music can music become significant to children.

In short, music must be considered at all levels, including the elementary level, as a *fine art*. It is its own excuse for being. It is not included in the curriculum as a means to some worthy but extra-musical end. Music in the elementary school is not *primarily* symbols on paper, nor nervous exhilaration nor recreation. It is a form of human behavior performed under special circumstances that is both unique and important to the individual.

Much of education from kindergarten to graduate school is highly verbal. The learner has a long and extended contact with words both in spoken and printed form. For the most part these verbal learnings concern concrete, specific things.

But the child also needs other experiences including those that words cannot express. Many of the great aesthetic experiences, especially in music, are far removed from verbalism. As Langer states it:

> . . . music is "significant form," and its significance is that of a symbol, a highly articulated sensuous object, which by virtue of its dynamic structure can express the forms of vital experience which language is peculiarly unfit to convey.[3]

Non-verbal, expressive communication is very much needed in the elementary school. None of the arts speaks so directly, intimately, and eloquently as music.

If one accepts the basic premise that art and music are fundamental to full and satisfactory living at every level of civilization, it should follow without argument that the arts are, properly, a concern of the school. They deserve a place not only in the elective areas of the curriculum but in the common core of the curriculum. Fortunately, in the elementary program, music is widely regarded as a learning of concern to *all* boys and girls.

Aims of Elementary Music Education

We may well agree that the primary aim of elementary music education is to contribute to the aesthetic growth and development of children. However, this lofty statement may seem removed by several light years from the day-by-day problems of actual teaching.

We need to enumerate some aims and clearly defined goals particularly applicable to the elementary music program. We do ourselves a disservice by making extravagant claims that music is as good as any subject and better than most in teaching such things as moral values, good health habits, and civic responsibility. Some of these learnings may indeed be attendant upon

[3] Susanne K. Langer, *Feeling and Form: A Theory of Art* (New York: Charles Scribner's Sons, 1953), p. 32.

music teaching but they are secondary, non-musical values. What we should be concerned about, primarily, is *musical* values and their significance to children in the elementary school. To be even more direct, we need to concern ourselves with the unique values that the study of music offers and the unique contributions it makes to personality fulfillment.

Music makes a *unique* contribution because the child develops an increasing aesthetic awareness and responsiveness through his experiences with tonal and rhythmic patterns that distinguish music from all other media. Perhaps a simpler way of saying the same thing is that musical experiences are unique because of the very nature of music itself. Because of its tonal-rhythmic organization, music is able to offer learning experiences that no other subject or activity in the elementary school is able to provide in precisely the same way.

Music makes an *important* contribution to growth because experiences in music are a part of the core experiences for all human beings. Music is important to all of us because, in varying degrees, music is an important part of our daily living.

The elementary child responds physically, emotionally, and intellectually to music. First and foremost, music is important to him as an individual. If general educators concur (and most do) that response to music is an important experience common to all human beings, there is no necessity for music educators to protest as much as we do in regard to the lack of recognition for music as a "respectable" subject. If we are able to show that music is important in the lives of all men, then we need do no more to justify its place in the daily schedule of the elementary school.

Values in Elementary Music Education

If we agree that music has unique and important contributions to make in the elementary program, we need to examine them. Although musical values may be categorized in many ways, it is necessary for us to consider the *intrinsic* as well as the *extrinsic* values of music teaching. Another way of saying this is that we need to provide, primarily, for *musical* values and, secondarily, for *extra-musical* values.

The *extrinsic* or extra-musical values of music include recreational, social, and enrichment values. These attributes have been well identified by music educators. They are important and they should continue to be emphasized. However, we should recognize that, of and by themselves, the extrinsic values cannot justify a program of music education in the public schools. If the only reason we schedule music is for fun, recreation, public relations and the like, we are basing our case on peripheral values. Both extrinsic and intrinsic values must be considered and provided for and it should be quite obvious, although it is too often ignored in practice, that the intrinsic values should be deliberately highlighted.

By *intrinsic* values, of course, we mean those learnings inherent in the music itself: tone, melody, rhythm, harmony, and form. Elementary music educators are coming to realize more and more clearly that these values need to be emphasized at least as fully as enrichment and recreational values. It seems very strange indeed that we need to recommend that we should teach something about music in a music program!

Intrinsic musical learnings include the ability of music to project mood, the characteristics of tone, and an introduction to rhythm, melody, harmony, and form. We shall be concerned with these in more detail later.

We have indicated that we have music in the schools because it makes a unique and important contribution to the growth and development of children. This is an answer that may appear very broad and even high-flown. Let us attempt some more direct answers that pinpoint explicitly some of the intrinsic as well as extrinsic values of music education:

1. We have music in the elementary school because music is a significant learning. Music has educational value in and of itself. It is a significant learning in its own right. Learning about music, listening to music, and making music are vital educational experiences deserving a place in the elementary schedule.

This is the first and foremost reason why we have music in the elementary program.

2. We have music in the elementary school because music provides pleasurable experiences. Simply stated, music must be *enjoyed.* Before we can expect youngsters to become vitally interested in music, they must want to participate because of the pleasure they receive. The child likes music because it makes him "feel good." There are many ways in which music gives enjoyment to children: singing with others, playing simple instruments, moving in response to music.

Music for fun, in the sense of pleasure for the moment, is only one phase of this objective. The ultimate goal should be deep and lasting satisfactions, noble and rewarding enjoyments, that come from real understandings and genuine responsiveness.

Some music educators have become almost apologetic that music can be a pleasurable experience. To de-emphasize the joy that music can bring to elementary children would be to ignore its major appeal to boys and girls.

3. We have music in the elementary school because music is rich in emotional values. Without belittling the intellectual aspects of music in any way, it is certainly true that one of the great appeals of music is its *emotional* impact. Music offers a way of expressing how one *feels.* It gives the student an opportunity to express the way he feels and of reacting to the way others feel. It can give him emotional release and satisfaction. In school activities, where intellectual achievement is generally the prime consideration, music provides an opportunity for emotional response that is of profound significance in individual development.

4. *We have music in the elementary school because music gives children opportunities for self-expression.* There are many opportunities in music-making for creative expression. Any performance of music is a process of re-creation. All musical activities—singing, playing, listening, or moving rhythmically—offer opportunities for creative expression. In addition, through such activities as "making up" additional verses to a tune, creating a simple melody of his own, or selecting the "right" percussive instruments to accompany class singing, the child has the opportunity to express himself in a way that is uniquely his own. It offers opportunities for expression that are quite different and beyond the routines that dominate so much of life, even in childhood. Music affords us one of the greatest joys attainable by man, the joy of creativity.

5. *We have music in the elementary school because music requires self-discipline.* That music is not only a pleasant vehicle for emotional release but that it can also be an exacting discipline is another of its special virtues. In the elementary school there is no expectation that the discipline will become as demanding as that required of the serious artist performer but there are disciplines that must be considered in even the most casual performance. Any performance of music from the most informal to the most artistic makes certain demands on the performer. The concern of the child to make his best possible contribution to solo or group performance represents a discipline of the highest order. To learn to work for and to achieve a desired end is a valuable learning.

6. *We have music in the elementary school because music promotes self-development.* In the area of self-development, music activities offer ample opportunities for achievement. Music has a great influence in shaping up one's attitudes, values, and aspirations.

One of the special attributes in music making is that there are so many "ceiling unlimited" opportunities for the child to go as far as his ability will carry him. This is especially important for the more able student although all children should be challenged to the limit of their capacities.

7. *We have music in the elementary school because music is a vital social force.* Music, by its very nature, is a social art. Musical activities offer many opportunities for establishing good social relationships. Through music, the child may be helped to achieve a place in the group. Subordinating individual desires to group goals and learning to cooperate purposefully with others are examples of how music serves as a socializing force in the classroom.

Significant music is created out of a human context. Its performance demands a social setting, for any art involves the sharing of human experience. Music in the classroom requires working with others.

8. We have music in the elementary school because music not only meets the present needs of children, it also develops new needs. That effective teaching meets the needs and interests of children and youth is a concept widely accepted. But the genius of teaching is not only in meeting present needs, but in creating new ones. In this connection, music serves to widen horizons, to deepen presently held insights as well as to explore completely new ideas.

Music offers an avenue for satisfying the natural curiosity that a child has concerning the world about him. It reinforces the child's present understandings and gives him the opportunity to explore entirely new learnings. Music leads children to an ever-growing awareness of the vast range and variety of human experience.

9. We have music in the elementary school because music enriches and supports other learnings. In addition to its own discipline, music can do much to intensify learnings in other areas (particularly in the social studies) through well-planned, integrated activities. Singing a song about a historical character makes him a more vivid personality to the child. An artistic musical setting of a fine poem highlights the beauty of the lyrics and intensifies the child's emotional response. A folk song of a people remote in time and place helps the child to "see" and understand them. Correlating music with other curriculum offerings is not only functional in the promotion of wider and deeper understandings in many subject areas, but these correlations also serve to indicate the many facets of music as a universal art form.

10. We have music in the elementary school because music offers a "change-of-pace" in classroom activities. Many experienced elementary teachers indicate that one of the great values of music in the daily program is the opportunity that music affords to add variety and zest to classroom activities. An opportunity to stretch muscles through singing games and folk dances, the possibility of listening quietly or singing vociferously as the occasion demands are examples of the widely varied activities that music can provide. When both minds and bodies are ready for a "change-of-pace," music can be of very real service to the creative teacher.

11. We have music in the elementary school not only because music is important in the "here-and-now" but also in later life as well. Much has been said about teaching "for today," but we need to be equally concerned with formulating attitudes toward music that will carry into adult life. That music, particularly listening to music, occupies a great part of the leisure hours of the adult American is a well-known fact. If the music program assumes little or no responsibility for developing appreciations that will last a lifetime, we are abdicating a primary responsibility. Music experiences and learnings not only enrich the present, but they also provide enrichment for all the years to come.

Music education in the elementary school is of prime importance to all music educators regardless of the level at which they happen to teach because it is *only* in the elementary school that we approach the ideal of music education as a common experience for every boy and girl. If the school music program is to make a significant impact on the school and its community, it has its greatest potential for doing so at the elementary level.

Summary

We concerned ourselves, first of all, with the broad aim of education: the optimum development of the individual as an effective, contributing member of our democratic way of life. We also observed that the primary aim of music education should be to discover how music experiences can contribute to the aesthetic growth of the individual within the setting of his culture.

The objectives of elementary music education were considered with an emphasis on the intrinsic values of music. Extrinsic values have great educative force but they are secondary rather than primary objectives of the music program.

Music deserves a place in the elementary curriculum because of the *unique* and *important* contribution it makes to personality fulfillment. Because of its tonal-rhythmic organization, music is able to provide learning experiences that are distinctive. To understand music, the elementary child must participate in making it.

We listed the following reasons why we have music in the elementary school:

Music is a significant learning.
Music provides pleasurable experiences.
Music is rich in emotional values.
Music gives children opportunities for self-expression.
Music invites self-discipline.
Music promotes self-development.
Music is a vital, social force.
Music meets present needs and develops new ones.
Music enriches and supports other learnings.
Music offers a welcome "change-of-pace."
Music is important now and in later life.

Finally, it was pointed out that it is only at the elementary level that we approach the ideal of music education in offering music activities as a common experience for every boy and girl in the school.

Questions for Discussion

1. Prepare a brief written statement giving your own views as to the broad objectives of education in today's schools.
2. Prepare a brief written statement giving your own views as to the broad objectives of elementary music education.
3. What does the statement "every person is a special kind of musician" mean?
4. Give examples of intrinsic values of music study; of extrinsic values. Are extrinsic values undesirable? Which should be emphasized?

5. Some philosophers take the position that music is not a language because it is non-verbal. Do you agree? What does music communicate?

6. Is the viewpoint that aesthetic experiences are *essentials* of life an over-statement? Why or why not?

7. In what sense is music a *unique* learning?

8. How is music a self-discipline?

9. Discuss the statement: "Music is a vital social force."

10. Give examples of how music might enrich other classroom learnings at the fifth grade level.

3

How Is Music Related
to Growth and Development?

"What are we teaching, music or children?"

It seems incredible that such an either-or proposition should have aroused such furor in music education a few years ago. At this writing, the divided forces appear to be coming closer together. We teach music *and* children and we are concerned about subject and learner simultaneously. The verb *learn* requires an object. We do not learn without learning *something*. We are not concerned with music alone but with music's relationship to the total and growing experience of the learner.

Any music teacher at any level is involved in a life-long study of music and of children. Part of the continuing fascination for all of us in the field is that there is no terminal point in the study of either music or children.

Unfortunately, music educators have not always been as ready to use the findings of developmental psychologists as teachers in other subject areas. The research in this area in the field of music teaching is quite limited and it is readily conceded that the observations made in this chapter are made on the basis of empirical study.

As we have already indicated, any basic aim or objective in education must be oriented to people. This is an obvious truism but far too many times we attempt to set up worthy objectives and aims that have very little relation to the needs, interests, capabilities, and limitations of boys and girls. The whole notion of "minimum essentials" becomes suspect if these essentials are considered apart from the individuals who are supposed to master them. To take a body of knowledge, to dissect it into a series of components which are then assigned arbitrarily to grade levels is a highly dangerous practice if the developmental abilities of the students are not taken into consideration.

The human material with which we work is the only resource whereby we can bring about any development through the process of education. The personality must be the starting point for all curriculum construction. One of our major problems in music education is to devise a curriculum that will be effective and appropriate at successive maturity levels. In order to build such a curriculum in music (or in any other subject area), it is fundamental that we have some understanding of how children grow and develop.

The curriculum has been defined as the total experience of a child for which the school is responsible. However, it is of importance that we also bear in mind that:

1. The curriculum is what a child *actually experiences* rather than what the school *intends* for him to experience.
2. Teachers, their personalities, and their attitudes to the child are important aspects of the curriculum.
3. Other children, what they say and do, how they feel about the child are a part of the curriculum.
4. The child's experiences outside school strongly affect his school experiences.
5. The child's unique abilities and limitations, his anxieties, and his adjustment problems either hinder or facilitate his learning experiences.

A fundamental aspect of curriculum making, then, is how human growth and development take place.

Research in the field indicates quite conclusively that learning, like behavior, is caused. Its causes, moreover, are not simple or singular. They are multiple, complex, and interrelated. Neither learning nor behavior "just happens." Let us consider some basic precepts for understanding the behavior of children.[1]

Fundamental Precepts

1. Behavior is caused and is meaningful. The way children behave, the reasons why they respond in the classroom as they do is of fundamental con-

[1] The precepts and the following six-area organizational framework are based on the writer's professional work with Dr. Daniel A. Prescott and his associates of the University of Maryland. They are outlined in Prescott's *The Child in the Educative Process* (New York: McGraw-Hill Book Company, Inc., 1957). Used by permission.

cern to all teachers. If Johnny behaves in a way that interferes with the on-going learnings of Mrs. Susan Crandall's class, the behavior does not "just happen." His loud talking, making faces, moving about the room unneces-sarily cause much confusion. *Why* does he behave as he does?

There is a cause for this behavior—or any other behavior. More ac-curately, there are multiple causes. To understand the behavior, Johnny's teacher must determine the causes.

Jim, through the years that Miss Carol Jones (the elementary music consultant) has known him, has indicated a consistent and apparently gen-uine interest in music. Yet, when invited to do so, he declines to sing in the school choir. Is his behavior without cause? Would not Miss Jones, like any good teacher, be at least curious to find out why Jim acts as he does?

2. *The causes which underlie behavior are complex, multiple, and in-terrelated.* Mrs. Crandall, Johnny's teacher, may decide on the basis of what she knows about Johnny that his unacceptable behavior in the classroom may be strictly for purposes of attracting attention. Conceding that this may be so, it is not the sole cause for the behavior. Johnny may act as he does because of limited attention given to him at home, or because he has re-cently moved and is "not at home" with his new peers, or he likes Mrs. Crandall, or he dislikes Mrs. Crandall, or he does not feel well, or because he is a high-energy child and cannot remain still for a prolonged period. The hypotheses for a specific act of behavior are many. The experienced teacher readily "smokes out" the more likely possibilities.

It is a fact that Jim does not want to sing in the choir. However, the causes are not always obvious. Jim may refuse to sing in the choir because his closest friend does not want to do so, or he prefers some other parallel enrichment activity offered, or he sings in an excellent church choir and already has a satisfactory choral experience, or he cannot accept the idea of being a "soprano," or he doesn't like the music, or he cannot stay after school for extra rehearsals because he rides the bus. Again, Miss Jones' task is to find what she believes to be the basic reasons and use these as a clue for understanding and possible action.

It is readily agreed that *all* of the reasons why a child behaves as he does may never be discovered. And it is readily conceded that the elementary music specialist has a particularly difficult task because of the large number of children with whom she works. But certainly it is vital that the elementary music specialist realize that there are many reasons why children behave as they do and it is part of her responsibility to search out some of the more likely ones and adjust her teaching procedures accordingly.

3. *Every child is worthy.* This is a statement that is so obvious that it seems unnecessary to state it at all. However, to accept every student as a worthy person regardless of background, dress, social class, or behavior re-quires all the knowledge, skill, and understanding that a teacher possesses.

Every child is valuable and has a right to those conditions, relationships, and experiences that will facilitate his development.

4. Every child is unique. The concept of individual differences is something we all know, all subscribe to, all believe, yet find extremely difficult to carry out in practice. Each individual is different from every other. No two children are alike yet many of us proceed in a manner that refutes the basic premise that each child is distinctly unique.

Children not only learn to read at different rates, but they also learn to read music at different rates. Children move at their own paces in developing number concepts as well as in apprehending the essentials of simple song form. Some fourth graders have great difficulty learning to spell while others have a real struggle coordinating the small finger muscles while playing the melody flute.

5. Every child is an indivisible entity. All of a child goes to school: his body, his mind, his spirit. He is a product of his heredity, conditioned by his environment. He brings to the music class his beliefs, his aspirations, his prejudices, and his fears. To not be at least partially aware of the many possible cross-currents that exert influences on him and his behavior is to overlook concerns of the first magnitude.

Admittedly, the elementary music specialist has a greater problem in coming to know children individually to the same extent that the classroom teacher knows and understands them. But the necessity for understanding children and probing for answers to the causes of behavior are as important to the music specialist, Miss Carol Jones, as to Mrs. Crandall, the fourth-grade teacher.

Setting up an organizational framework to study children in a developmental program offers many insights in planning a music program to meet the developmental skills, interests, and needs of children at successive maturity levels. This organizational framework includes six areas: (1) the physical processes; (2) the affectional processes; (3) the socialization processes; (4) the peer group processes; (5) the self-developmental processes; and (6) the self-adjustive processes.

Major Developmental Areas

1. Physical Processes. To the developmental psychologist, physical factors include such processes as growth rate, maturity level, energy output, state of health, rhythm of activity and rest, physical limitations, and general appearance.

These have obvious implications for music teachers. Physiological maturation of small muscles largely determines when the child can begin to use flute-like instruments. Control of his body determines how soon the child may effectively participate in patterned dances. The high-energy output of most elementary children is responsible for the great attention given to physical responses to music in the elementary grades. The developmental refinement of motor coordination must be kept in mind in planning music experiences in grades one through six. The earlier maturation of girls poses special problems for the elementary specialist, particularly in the upper elementary grades.

2. *Affective Processes.* Affective processes include the relationships of the child with his parents, brothers and sisters, close friends, his teacher, and other persons who sincerely value the child and provide him with a feeling of emotional security and well-being.

We are beginning to realize more and more clearly that the emotional climate of a learning situation determines in large measure how efficiently the child will learn facts and master skills. The role of music as an expressive vehicle able to transmit and convey feelings and emotions is generally well known, but is not always duly recognized by practicing music educators.

3. *Socialization Processes.* The child's socialization processes include influences of the family, community institutions such as the church, clubs and recreational facilities, the school itself, the culture of the area in which the child lives, the influence of geography and of social class, and the ethnic group to which the child belongs.

The role of music in the socialization process is enormously important. The kind of music heard in the home, in the church, and in various community music organizations all exert a very real influence upon the socialization processes of the child. One of the great challenges in music education is the necessity for more closely relating the music the child experiences in the school to the mainstream of cultural influence in his home and community. Conversely, music in the school should exert a positive influence on home and community.

4. *Peer-group Processes.* The peer group includes the child's classmates and other age-mates outside the classroom. We are interested in the child's role in the group, the status accorded him, his successes and failures in seeking desirable group roles, and how he goes about winning the approval of the group. We are interested in determining whether the child is a leader or a follower, whether he is accepted, isolated, or a fringe member of his group.

Music, because of its involvement of groups, can do much to help the child earn group acceptance. Some children may be able to win recognition and leadership roles in music activities that they might not achieve in other subjects. Any performance of music offers possibilities that will help the child to establish satisfactory peer relationships.

5. *Self-development Processes.* In the self-development area we are concerned with the child's conception of himself, his conception of his society, the feelings he has about others and about the world, his aptitudes and limitations, his skills, interests, attitudes and his immediate as well as his

long-range goals and aspirations. We are concerned in the development of those self-characteristics that distinguish the child as a unique member of his group.

The child's discovery of the power and beauty of music can be a vital factor in self-development. The youngster needs and desires (to a degree which we may never fully appreciate) experiences which feed and strengthen his growing self. We need, almost desperately, to do something in our educational program to help children acquire realistic attitudes of self-acceptance. Music can make contributions in terms of the child's understanding of self and his world as well as sharpening his perceptions of his ideals and aspirations.

6. *Self-adjustment Processes.* Self-adjustment involves the child's feelings about his physical adequacy, his appraisal of his affectional relationships, his attitudes toward his social acceptance, his estimate of his role among his peers, and his total evaluation of his adequacy as an effective personality. We are concerned in helping the child learn self-adjustment mechanisms that assist him in maintaining his equilibrium.

Again, music can be of help in solving self-adjustment problems. Music experiences can do much for the child's feelings of happiness and can add to his adequacy, security, achievement, acceptance, and sense of belonging. It is certainly not too much to presume that some children may be affected by their contacts and insights with music in such a way as to bring about a more positive appraisal of self.

Developmental Characteristics

What implications do growth and development principles have for the teaching of music in the elementary school? Is this not all pedagogical theory far removed from the basal music text, the staff-liner, and the pitch pipe?

We have been remiss in not adapting the findings and research of the developmental psychologists more directly to teaching music. At the risk of over-simplifying the problem, an attempt is made in the following pages to sketch an outline of developmental maturation of boys and girls in the elementary school and relating it to an orderly sequence of music activities at each grade level.

Grade I

The six-year-old child	*Music activities in the first grade*
is growing at his unique rate. Although there may be a range of less than one year in chronological age within the	offer a wide variety of experiences to meet the needs, interests, and readiness of children of varying maturity levels.

class, there may be several years of difference in physical maturation.

has extremely high energy output, enjoys rough and tumble games and other vigorous physical activity.	offer many opportunities for the release of physical energy through free movement, rhythms, games, songs, and dances.
enjoys spontaneous play.	encourage free, creative physical responses in interpreting songs and recordings.
has larger muscles that are more advanced in development and control than the small muscles of hands and fingers.	involve the use of the larger muscles, the whole body. Finger play provides experiences in developmental control of smaller muscles.
enjoys using his hands.	provide for clapping, tapping, and other hand movements; include the playing of simple melody and rhythm instruments as well as keyboard experience.
requires a balance of rest and activity.	include quiet songs and listening periods as well as physical activity.
has eyes that are not yet mature; there is a tendency in most six-year-olds toward far-sightedness.	emphasize a "by-ear" rather than a "by-eye" approach to musical understanding. Charts and large scale notes are used.
is highly egocentric.	feature many songs about himself, his games, his toys, his clothes.
is very much home-centered.	include songs about the home and family.
is interested in pets and animals.	include songs about animals.
chooses a best friend from the same sex.	should include songs about friendship and social relationships.
is concerned about finding his role in the new school situation.	help him feel "at home" in the classroom through singing familiar songs and taking part in familiar games.
is interested in the immediate, the here-and-now.	provide song texts that stress the immediacy of the child's world.
likes to assume responsibility.	give him such responsibilities as being the leader in a singing game, playing a rhythm instrument, getting out and putting away music materials.
finds decisions, choices hard to make.	surround the child with rich, musical activities but defer the making of many discriminative choices. However, some choices should be made that are within his understanding.
is developing a sense of humor.	include fun and nonsense songs.

Grade II

The seven-year-old child	*Music activities in the second grade*
is growing at his unique rate. Although there may be a range of less than one year in chronological age within the class, there may be several years of difference in physical maturation.	offer a wide variety of experiences to meet the needs, interests, and readiness of children of varying maturity levels.
has high energy output and enjoys physical activity.	offer many opportunities for the release of physical energy in games, dances, songs, and rhythms.
enjoys dramatic play, makes up things naturally and spontaneously.	encourage free, creative physical responses in interpreting songs and recordings.
has larger muscles that are in advance of development of smaller muscles of the hands and fingers.	involve the use of the larger muscles, the whole body.
enjoys using his hands.	provide opportunities for hand movement; playing instruments, clapping, and "shaping" the melody.
may tire easily, may show fatigue late in the school day.	include quiet songs and listening periods as well as physical activity.
has eyes that are not ready to accommodate close-at-hand work for extended periods.	emphasize a "by-ear" rather than a "by-eye" approach to musical understanding. Charts and large scale notes are used.
is very self-centered.	include songs about himself, his body, his toys, pets, clothes.
is competitive, wants to be first.	should provide opportunities for shifting leadership roles frequently in group music activities.
is beginning to reach out to a wider world beyond his home and family.	should include songs about his neighborhood, his community, his country.
is seeking adult and peer-mate approval; is anxious to please, to do well.	provide many opportunities for success and achievement.
still lives, for the most part, in the immediate present. He finds it difficult to plan for the future.	provide song texts that stress the immediacy of the child's world.
is able, however, to carry learnings over to the next day.	offer some learning experiences that require a greater period of time than one class session. Most learnings, however, may be grasped at once.

is able to assume more responsibility than the six-year-old child.

provide increased opportunities for leadership roles in music activities as well as increased responsibilities in caring for music materials, instruments, and equipment.

has a sense of humor.

include fun and nonsense songs.

Grade III

The eight-year-old child	*Music activities in the third grade*
is growing at his unique rate. Although there may be a range of less than one year in chronological age within the class, there may be several years of difference in physical maturation.	offer a wide variety of experiences to meet the needs, interests, and readiness of children of varying maturity levels.
has high energy output, is very active, is less fatigable.	offer many opportunities for the release of physical energy.
enjoys strenuous physical activity.	provide directed experiences to capitalize on this interest in games, dances, and rhythms.
is gaining better control of the small muscles of hands and fingers, has improved eye-hand coordination.	provide many opportunities for playing simple melody and rhythm instruments. However, flute-like instruments are best deferred until the fourth grade.
has eyes that are ready for close-up as well as distant work.	provide for increased attention to and study of the musical score.
requires a rhythm of activity and rest.	include quiet songs and listening periods as well as activities featuring free movement, singing games, and dances.
participates readily in group activities, is beginning to form group or gang relationships.	emphasize group participation, provide activities that foster group acceptance.
is becoming less dependent on the teacher.	offer increased opportunities for independence in music-making; e.g., playing the autoharp.
is increasingly aware of individual differences: that his classmates do some things better than he; that he excels in others.	provide for individual differences, offer many opportunities to shift leadership roles in group music activities.
is beginning to extend his life-space, his environment.	include songs with texts reflecting his expanding interests beyond his immediate community.
has a better understanding of time. He is also interested in the "long ago" as well as the present.	include songs involving time concepts and songs dealing with historical persons and events.

is gaining skill in reading fluently. Enjoys poetry.

emphasize lyrics, intensify music reading experiences.

makes up things naturally and spontaneously.

encourage creative responses in singing, playing, moving, and listening.

is eager to learn, is willing to take on new experiences.

provide opportunities to explore many new facets of melody, rhythm, harmony, and form.

begins to tell jokes, to enjoy humorous situations.

include fun and nonsense songs.

is beginning to develop a sense of loyalty.

provide appropriate songs dealing with patriotism, devotion, and loyalty.

Grade IV

The nine-year-old child

Music activities in the fourth grade

is growing at his unique rate. At this level the growth of girls is accelerating. Some girls may be several years ahead of the boys in physical maturation. There may be a range of from four to six years in physical maturation in one class.

are widely varied to meet the needs and interests of children of varying maturity. Although group work continues to be emphasized, more opportunities are provided for individual participation.

is not so continuously active as children in the primary grades, requires a rhythm of activity and rest.

although continuing to provide many opportunities for physical responses, give more time to the study of music where bodily movement is not of prime consideration.

has good control of his body, has finer coordination.

include not only fundamental rhythms but games and dances with organized, patterned movement.

has eyes that are almost mature, has good eye-hand coordination.

provide increased attention to the reading of notation. Introduce the use of flute-like instruments and recorders.

is becoming less dependent on adults.

offer many outlets for independence in performing and listening to music.

is very much concerned about acceptance by his peers. Clubs and gangs are even stronger than in the third grade.

provide many opportunities for group involvement and group acceptance.

is gaining increasing independence in reading. There may be a span in reading ability of four or five years in the classroom.

offer a wide variety of reading experiences. Learnings must be presented in cyclical rather than cumulative fashion. All children should not be expected to have equal proficiency in reading music.

is continuing to extend the horizons of his everyday world.

should include songs about people in other times, other places.

is interested in the past and the future as well as the present.

should include songs with texts reflecting this broadened interest.

is interested in heroic personalities.

should include texts dealing with real and legendary heroes.

has a good sense of humor.

include fun and nonsense songs.

makes up things naturally and spontaneously.

should encourage creative responses in singing, playing, moving, and listening to music.

is becoming increasingly concerned with skills and techniques.

emphasize greater skill in singing and playing.

has a longer attention span than primary children.

provide for more extended songs, longer listening periods.

welcomes reasonable explanations, does not want to be talked-down-to.

should present musical learnings in precise language. The technical aspects of music should be stated in simple but accurate terms.

is tremendously curious about what makes things work.

should provide an introduction to the more elementary aspects of how sound is produced.

is capable of making his own decisions.

provide greater opportunities for making discriminative choices.

is creative.

encourage creative responses in singing, playing, moving, and listening to music.

is becoming aware of his spiritual needs.

include songs from our sacred heritage appropriate for this level.

Grade V

The ten-year-old child

Music activities in the fifth grade

is growing at his unique rate. A few early maturers are entering the pre-adolescent growth spurt. Late maturers exhibit growth pattern of late childhood. There may be a range in physical maturity from four to six years in this grade.

are widely varied to meet the needs and interests of children of varying maturity. Although group work is emphasized, individual participation in classroom music permits the child to function at his maturity level.

has good control of his body although early maturers may indicate occasional fatigue and show a lack of coordination.

provide not only a wide variety of physical activities but periods of relaxation and quiet listening.

has eyes that are well-developed, has good eye-hand coordination.

continue to emphasize reading and use of melody and rhythm instruments. Many students are ready for orchestra and band instruments.

is increasingly less dependent on adults, may resist adult authority.

offer outlet for independence in performing and listening to music.

needs emotional security. This is especially true of the pre-adolescent.

provide many opportunities for emotional identification and realization.

is increasingly interested in skills and techniques.

emphasize skill in singing and playing.

is becoming more interested in the opposite sex.

include songs such as dialogue songs that treat boy-girl relationships in a positive way, include folk-dancing and square dancing.

is a fluent reader. Reading ability may span four or five years in one class.

provide for the presentation of reading experiences in cyclical rather than cumulative fashion. One should expect a wide range in the ability of children to read.

is increasingly interested in the affairs of his community, his country, the world.

include songs from many regions of our country, from other lands.

is strongly influenced by out-of-school music activities.

are planned recognizing the influence of radio, television, the movies, and community music programs.

has a longer attention span.

include longer, more complex songs, provide longer listening selections.

welcomes reasonable explanations, does not want to be talked-down-to.

present musical learnings in precise language. The technical aspects of music should be stated in simple but accurate terms.

has a good sense of humor.

include fun and nonsense songs.

is interested in heroic personalities, great men.

include songs about heroes, real and legendary.

is interested in work and occupations.

provide work songs appropriate for the fifth grade.

likes to do things well.

encourage the child to perform to the best of his ability—there is no "ceiling" on musical enrichment.

is capable of making his own decisions.

offer opportunities for making discriminative choices.

is creative.

encourage creative responses in singing, playing, moving, and listening to music.

needs to succeed, to belong, to be accepted.

provide many opportunities for socialized involvement and interaction; encourage achievement, success, belonging.

is becoming aware of his spiritual needs.

include songs from our sacred heritage appropriate for this level.

Grade VI

The eleven-year-old child	*Music activities in the sixth grade*
is growing at his unique rate. Early maturers are entering the pre-adolescent growth spurt. Girls indicate more individual variations in physical structure than boys. Late maturers exhibit the growth patterns of late childhood. There may be a range in physical maturity from four to six years in this grade.	are widely varied to meet the needs and interests of children of varying maturity. Although group work is emphasized, individual participation in classroom music activities permits the child to function at his maturity level.
is active, has good control of his body. He may indicate fatigue because of his rapid growth.	provide a wide variety of physical responses from free movement to dances with highly organized patterns; include quiet songs and listening periods.
enjoys sports and outdoor play, particularly organized team activity. This is especially true of boys but also true of girls.	provide directed experiences in games and dances. Elementary choirs, bands, and orchestras provide outlets for team spirit and cooperation.
has good eye-hand coordination.	continue to emphasize the use of melody and rhythm instruments. The recorder is especially appropriate. Many students are playing band and orchestra instruments.
may begin to develop secondary sex characteristics.	may reveal a deepening, richer quality in the voices of some girls. A very few boys' voices may begin to change.
is less dependent on adults.	offer outlets for independence in performing and listening to music.
realizes that, regardless of personal wishes, he must accept his responsibility to the group.	offer many opportunities to learn to subordinate individual desires for group goals. This is self-discipline of the highest order.
is becoming more interested in the opposite sex.	include many songs, such as dialogue songs, that treat girl-boy relationships in a positive manner.
is a fluent reader.	provide for a summation of reading learnings presented in the earlier grades. The student is expected to develop some modest reading facility.
is increasingly concerned about the affairs of the community, the nation, the world.	include songs from many regions, other lands.

is aware of and influenced by music heard out-of-school.	are planned recognizing the influence of radio, the movies, television, and community music programs. Guidance is provided for his after-school music activities.
has a longer attention span.	include longer, more complex songs; provide longer extracts from standard literature in listening periods.
vacillates between late childhood and early adolescent roles.	include songs with a wide range of interest and appeal.
has a good sense of humor.	include fun and nonsense songs.
is interested in heroic personalities, great men.	include songs about heroes, real and legendary.
is interested in work and occupations.	include work songs appropriate for this level.
likes to do things well.	encourage the child to perform to the best of his ability.

Implications for the Music Specialist

Of what concern are developmental characteristics to the elementary music specialist? How can Miss Carol Jones, who teaches approximately one thousand children every week, come to know more than a few children as individual personalities?

Any teacher of any subject at any level *must* know a very great deal about the children with whom she works or she will not succeed. It is true that in many ways children are unique. However, it is also true that in many ways children are alike.

Miss Jones will come to know only a few children well. However, she will have the advantage of seeing children over a number of years and in circumstances that are not restricted to academic situations. Although she may not know many fourth-grade children as well as does Mrs. Crandall, the fourth-grade teacher, she will come to know the generalized abilities and limitations of fourth graders in music in several classrooms very well indeed. The necessity for being well aware of the physical, affectional, peer culture, socialization, self-developmental, and self-adjustive factors of children at a given maturity level is of great importance to the elementary music specialist.

If Miss Jones hopes to help children grow musically, it should be obvious that she must know a very great deal about music. It should be equally obvious that if she hopes to help children grow musically, she also must know a very great deal about the developmental characteristics of children.

A highly significant point is that the more the music consultant learns about how children behave and learn the more she will understand how adults behave and learn. To provide for personality differences among her thirty elementary teachers is every bit as important a working ideal for Miss Jones as it is for Mrs. Crandall to provide for individual differences in her classroom.

Summary

In this chapter we have been concerned with relating the findings of developmental psychology to the teaching of music. We discussed certain basic axioms of human behavior, and then we considered the six-area organizational framework that included physical processes, affectional processes, socialization processes, peer-group processes, self-developmental processes, and self-adjustment processes.

Finally, we listed certain developmental characteristics by grade level and related them to the musical activities and experiences that are implied.

Music teaching involves a life-long study of music and children. Neither study has a terminal point.

Questions for Discussion

1. What does the term "child growth and development" mean to professional educators? Why should music educators avail themselves of the findings of the developmental psychologists?
2. Why is the notion of "minimum essentials" suspect?
3. How might the curriculum in a study guide differ sharply from the curriculum the child experiences?
4. Discuss the statement: "All behavior is caused and is meaningful."
5. What is meant by *affective processes?* What contributions may music education make in this area?
6. What is the *peer culture?*
7. Give examples of self-development processes, of self-adjustment processes. What are their implications for music teaching?
8. Select one of the elementary grades and the list of developmental characteristics as set forth in this chapter. Can you extend the list of implied music activities? Can you suggest other developmental characteristics and their implications for music teaching?
9. Does an understanding of behavioral psychology have application for the elementary music consultant in working with elementary teachers?
10. What is meant by the "growth spurt"? When does it usually occur?

4

The Aims of
Elementary Music Supervision

Just as it is essential to establish general objectives of education before one may formulate aims for a special field, it is necessary to be familiar with the principles of supervision before one may attempt to set specific goals for elementary music supervision. We may gain some insight into general supervisory practices by considering two questions: (1) what is the purpose of supervision? and (2) what does a supervisor do?

Anyone entering the field of educational supervision soon becomes aware that there is limited research to support working procedures. There is a need for studies to support and refine current practices as well as to suggest additional ways of working. This applies not only to the field of general supervision but to music supervision as well.

The theory of supervision is still in a state of evolution. At one time, supervision was considered to be an inspecting, directing, and judging activity. The supervisor told teachers what to do, showed them how to do it, and then followed up to see how well his instructions were carried out.

Today the supervisor seeks to achieve an improved teaching-learning situation by working cooperatively with teachers in an assisting, sharing role. In working toward this goal, the supervisor serves in many ways.

What Does an Instructional Supervisor Do?

1. The constant objective of supervision is to bring about an improvement of learning. Of course, it is impossible for the supervisor to approach this goal through his own efforts. It is necessary for teachers, principals and administrators to become involved if an effective program of curriculum improvement is to be initiated and developed. How well the supervisor succeeds depends on his effectiveness in working with people.

The supervisor stimulates, coordinates, and guides professional growth. The ultimate objective is to improve the skills, competencies, and insights that teachers acquire so that they will be able to provide more effective learning experiences for their students.

At the elementary level the general supervisor of instruction is usually concerned with language arts, mathematics, science and the social studies.

However, he should be as concerned about the expressive arts as he is for other areas of the elementary curriculum.

2. The supervisor provides effective educational leadership. He is an *official* leader in terms of his appointment by the superintendent. He is a *recognized* leader to the extent that recognition is given to him by the teacher group. It is possible for the supervisor to attempt to dominate the group, to have teachers work *for him*. Or, he may see his function only as a service to help the group carry out its purposes, to work *for teachers*. But most supervisors see themselves as working *with* a group, helping them to identify problems and formulate aims, working within the group to achieve established goals. Ideally, the supervisor *works with* teachers.

The democratic approach recognizes that in many endeavors the supervisor may not be the only person qualified to serve as group leader. The supervisor does all he can to further the development of emergent leadership from the group of teachers he serves. To promote, to recognize, and to permit emergent leadership to function is a distinguishing trait of the democratic leader.

3. Since the supervisor can bring about curriculum improvement only by working with people, he realizes that he must display warmth and friendliness. Teachers want to feel comfortable about their work, they want to be treated fairly, they want to be recognized for their contributions, and they want to participate in making policy decisions that affect them.

The supervisor can be instrumental in bringing about the desired working climate that is necessary if professional growth is to take place. He does so by being readily available when help is needed. He is sensitive to work on problems as teachers see them.

Any change in curriculum will not be realized until a change has occurred in people. As Miel puts it, "curriculum change should be seen for what it really is—a type of social change, change in people, not mere change on paper."[1]

4. The supervisor helps the teacher gain greater competencies. This does not mean that the supervisor is an omniscient person, knowing all things and able to solve all problems. He brings about improvement in instruction by drawing on the resources of teachers, administrators, and outside consultants. He may achieve this goal partially through classroom observations, through individual conferences, by arranging for demonstration lessons, through group meetings, workshops, inter-visitations, principals' meetings and the like.

5. He helps evaluate the program. Again, the supervisor must involve others in the process. Although there are many criteria, the supervisor is primarily concerned with evidences of more efficient teaching and learning. He looks for enrichments and extensions of curriculum offerings. He judges the effectiveness of teaching, in large measure, by responses of children. He also looks for evidence that indicates whether the school is adequately meeting the needs of the community it serves.

Implicit in any process of evaluation is a reappraisal of goals and objectives. Both strengths and weaknesses are assessed and steps for further improvement are charted.

6. He helps interpret the program. The general supervisor is in an advantageous position to interpret the educational program to the public. He has frequent opportunities to speak before civic clubs and community groups. He serves as a liaison with community agencies. In many ways, he is probably more familiar with the overall program of instruction than other school administrators. As a result, he is often sought out as a spokesman for the school's instructional program.

In addition, the general supervisor is in a unique position to hear what the public expects of its schools. One has only to attend a luncheon club as a representative schoolman to find how true this is. To be sensitive to public opinion is an important aspect of the supervisor's interpretive function.

Implications for Elementary Music Supervision

The elementary music consultant is guided by the same principles and procedures as the general supervisor. Every one of the points made for the general supervisor applies to the specialist supervisor as well. However, in some ways, the nature of the music consultant's job and the objectives established require different ways of working.

1. Without question, the primary mission of the elementary music con-

---

[1] Alice Miel, *Changing the Curriculum, A Social Process* (New York: Appleton-Century-Crofts, 1946), p. 10.

sultant is to improve the quality of musical experiences in the elementary school. However, it is extremely important that the consultant view the music program in its relationship to the total educational endeavor. The more she knows about the basic program, the better she is able to plan and carry out a satisfactory program of music education.

After several years of experience, the music consultant usually becomes well aware of the basic learning experiences for each grade level. She also is aware of those activities where music may make a contribution. Frequent individual conferences with teachers, attendance at faculty meetings and in-service study groups will give the consultant added insight into the curriculum focus of the classes of teachers she serves.

Like the general supervisor, the music consultant realizes that she cannot hope to bring about instructional improvement through her own efforts. The cooperation of teachers, principals, and administrators is essential.

2. *The role of the elementary music consultant as an educational leader is somewhat different from that of the instructional supervisor.* The elementary music consultant usually has less *official* leadership status than does the general supervisor. Ordinarily she is not a member of the central office staff nor does she have a peer relationship with principals and general supervisors. She is usually considered to have a direct peer relationship with teachers. She often has a working title other than supervisor. We have referred to her as the elementary music consultant. She may also be known as an elementary music supervisor, helping teacher, resource teacher, special teacher, or coordinator.

The elementary music consultant must work hard to develop *recognized* leadership—leadership given to her by the group of teachers she serves, leadership earned by the quality of her service. To a greater extent than the general supervisor, she must *work with* teachers rather than attempting to get them to work *for her.* She must also be alert for any clues or signs indicating that some teachers are prepared and willing to assume leadership functions in the elementary music program.

3. *The elementary music consultant, too, must do everything possible to establish a warm, friendly working environment.* Many teachers feel insecure about teaching music and will not be comfortable with the consultant in their classroom until they know that she is there to help and to guide rather than to inspect and judge.

On this point Wiles makes the following observation:

> The special subject supervisor's success depends upon competency in his field and his way of working with people. If he does not show insight in his discussions with principals and staff, he will be ignored. He cannot succeed simply because he bears the label supervisor. If he does not present his ideas in a friendly, relaxed manner, he will not be taken seriously or called again. We build defenses against someone who threatens us by his manner or by use of his knowledge. *The supervisor's*

participation must convince others that his knowledge is a tool at their service rather than a club to force conformity to a pattern they cannot understand or accept.[2]

The elementary music consultant may be junior to most classroom teachers in both years and experience. She must literally prove herself to them (rather than vice versa) before she will be accepted. Teachers expect two things of the consultant: (1) competency in the field of music, and (2) a warm, sympathetic, helpful way of working with them.

4. The elementary music consultant helps the classroom teacher gain skills, understandings, and competencies.

There is a wide range in preparation, training, and interests of elementary teachers in music—perhaps an even greater range than for the so-called "academic" subject areas. Whereas every teacher will have had minimal pre-service preparation in the language arts, mathematics, science, and the social sciences, it is possible in some situations for her to be certified as an elementary teacher with no pre-service work in music education. Elementary teachers feel very strongly that the music consultant brings to the job considerable background, skill, and training in music. They feel that her primary mission is to strengthen their musical background and help them with their teaching.

Specific Aims

Thus far we have indicated parallel aims that both the general supervisor and the specialist supervisor have in common. However, we also need to examine aims that are particularly applicable to the music program at the elementary level.

The elementary music consultant endeavors:

1. To encourage every teacher to include music in the daily program. This is certainly not a profound, philosophical aim. It is, however, a very practical and a most necessary one. It is the height of folly to talk about improving the program of music in a classroom where there is no program to improve!

The first aim of the music consultant should be to do everything possible to encourage the classroom teacher to make a real effort to teach music when the specialist is not present. The music activities in some rooms may be very modest. To begin with, they may include little more than an "opening" song and an occasional non-directed listening period.

Early in her consultant work, Miss Carol Jones found that she was overwhelming some teachers with her well-rehearsed description of the complete, comprehensive music program. To a teacher like Miss Edith Allen, the expectation that she is to have her children move to music and sing and play and listen and read and create seems an impossible undertaking.

[2] Kimball Wiles, *Supervision for Better Schools* (Englewood Cliffs, N. J.: Prentice-Hall, Inc., 1955), p. 154.

Actually, what Miss Allen or any "musically timid" teacher needs in the beginning is *success* in some music activity, literally *any* kind of music activity. If she will make an attempt this school year to present listening experiences for her six-year-olds, Miss Jones should feel that significant progress has been made. Teachers should be given the opportunity to start with an activity where they feel secure and where they believe they can succeed. There are many avenues to musical learning. No one has yet been able to establish any clear-cut "best way" to teach music in the elementary classroom.

2. *To improve the music teaching skills of elementary teachers.* The elementary music consultant is concerned with the musicality of the teacher and, ultimately, of her pupils. Ideally, the consultant would hope to work with teachers so effectively and so efficiently that, eventually, her services would no longer be required.

This Utopian goal will be achieved with only a few unusually competent teachers. However, as a basic method of operation, Miss Carol Jones works with teachers in such a way that they will achieve a modest measure of musical independence over the years.

As a specific illustration, we may cite the case of Miss Allen and her interest in percussive instruments for the first grade. It is one thing for Miss Carol Jones to teach Miss Allen's *children* how to handle the percussive instruments to accompany singing, movement, or recordings. Working as the direct teacher, Miss Jones will need to repeat the instruction year after year. But if Miss Jones approaches the problem with the primary intent of teaching *Miss Allen* how to handle rhythm instruments as one phase of her teaching, it is quite a different matter. Not everything can be accomplished in one year. However, with Miss Jones' guidance, Miss Allen will be less and less dependent on the consultant.

In improving music teaching skills, Miss Jones is as interested in musical learnings as she is in activities. It is not only important that music be included in the daily schedule, but also equally important that musical activities be of worth and integrity and that they offer something of significance to boys and girls.

3. *To help clarify the shared responsibilities of consultant, teacher, and principal as they relate to the music program.* There is abundant evidence that administrators and general supervisors feel that the special areas are important in the elementary school and that teachers need resource help. Specialists are employed to provide this help, yet often they are employed without a clear-cut understanding as to their function. It is as though the administrator says, "We have hired you. We're not quite sure just what it is we want you to do. But do something!"

Unfortunately, this is not an exaggeration. This condition exists in far too many systems. This poses a difficult situation for the music consultant. It is awkward for her to talk objectively about her job to people with whom she is associated in a service capacity.

To clarify the responsibilities of consultant, teacher, and principal is an important and continuing concern of elementary music supervision. There is much that the elementary music consultant can do but there are also many problems that cannot be solved without the active involvement of teacher and principal. For example, the consultant cannot demand that teachers remain in the classroom when they have become accustomed to regard her visit as a "coffee break." This is a problem that the principal must be concerned about before any satisfactory solution can be made. The main obstacle to achieving a clarification of the respective responsibilities of teacher, consultant, and principal is indifference on the part of one or more of the parties concerned as to the role of music in elementary education.

4. *To develop, cooperatively, a balanced, coordinated program of music education.* The elementary music consultant, naturally, should be expected to have a great deal to say about the organization, content, and sequence of the elementary music program. But this does not mean that she will "go it alone" and dole out the learnings piece-meal in an authoritative way.

There are a number of things that the consultant must keep in mind. First, she must have an understanding of the objectives of elementary education. Second, she must have in mind realistic expectancies for the music education program. Third, she must have the musical knowledge, understanding, and skill required. Fourth, she must have an understanding of the developmental capabilities and limitations of children.

In the realization of these objectives, the elementary teacher and the principal can be of invaluable help to the consultant. If it is recognized that Miss Jones brings to the task a depth of understanding in music that exceeds that of the elementary teacher, it must also be recognized that the elementary teacher will know more about the developmental characteristics of boys and girls at a given level. If Miss Jones is a specialist in terms of her understanding of music, Mrs. Crandall is also a specialist in her understanding of nine-year-old boys and girls in her fourth-grade class.

5. *To be aware that music can enrich, support, and reinforce other learnings.* In order to see the possibilities for direct correlation with other areas, the consultant must know as much as possible about the general classroom program. It is highly desirable that the music consultant know the grade-level expectancies in the language arts, mathematics, science, and the social studies. This is a difficult but not an impossible objective.

The very appearance of many classrooms literally shouts the central theme or topic of study. It does not take an unusually perceptive person visiting a fifth-grade classroom that features a table covered with products and handicrafts of Mexico, murals of Mexican life, posted essays on Mexican history, and a reading assignment on the chalkboard concerning Mexican agriculture to suspect that a few Mexican songs would be welcomed by the teacher.

The social studies, in particular, offer many possibilities for correlation. However, the language arts and, to a lesser degree, the sciences also offer enrichment opportunities.

6. To interpret the goals and values of the elementary music program. The consultant interprets the music program to both professionals and laymen. Perhaps her work in clarifying goals and values with educators is at least as important as her efforts in doing so with school patrons.

The consultant should have a clear understanding of the distinctive aesthetic contribution music makes to the developing personality. She should point out that this is consistent with the broad aim of education. Although she is happy to seize on the recreational and social values that music offers, she indicates in every way she can that these are secondary rather than primary values.

One of her most effective ways of interpreting values is not in what she *says* so much as in what she *does*. If growing music responsiveness is held up as a primary objective, then we would expect music in the elementary school to be of high quality, appropriate for the level, and centered on musical values. The principal would find it hard to understand Miss Carol Jones' viewpoint if she indicated verbally that musicality is her central theme when he observes that she spends nearly all of her time on fun songs of dubious value. The elementary music consultant can best interpret the program to teachers, principals, and administrators by the way she performs her job.

One group of educators that the elementary music consultant should not overlook are members of the music staff assigned to the secondary level. It is a very good plan for the entire music staff of the school system to assemble periodically to discuss responsibilities, problems, and procedures. Secondary school music teachers need to know about the elementary program. Elementary music specialists can do a more effective job if their efforts are coordinated with the music program of the secondary school. Since growth in musical responsiveness is a central aim for all, there is much common ground for system-wide music staff conferences.

As far as patrons are concerned, parents of elementary children will be much more interested in the music program than other people in the community. However, if parents develop positive feelings toward the music program, these feelings will persist long after their children have completed their elementary schooling.

Miss Carol Jones needs to plan performances that have an entertainment emphasis. These include such programs as the Christmas-carol sing, the auditorium program for "go-to-school" night, and a demonstration of folk dances for the P.T.A. However, it is still important that she focus on the interests and concerns of children in preference to the interests and concerns of the adult audience. Parents are most agreeable to this emphasis if they are informed about it. Even in a somewhat formal program, parents appreciate hearing an explanation as to why the children are engaged in a specific activity, what they hope to accomplish, and how the activity relates to the total school program.

As one specific suggestion, opportunities should be provided for observations of music experiences *in the classroom*. For example, on "go-to-school" night, the parents of Mrs. Crandall's fourth-grade children will enjoy a program of folk songs accompanied by simple instruments in the natural classroom setting more than a formal program on the auditorium stage.

The music specialist will not ordinarily have extensive contacts with community patrons who do not have children in the elementary school. She may be asked, however, to perform such tasks as working with the symphony board on children's programs, conducting the elementary choir at civic meetings, preparing talks for various groups, and, perhaps, doing an occasional demonstration on radio or television.

Such opportunities, to the extent that they do not interfere with the consultant's basic professional mission, are excellent for interpreting the elementary music program. However, there is an ever-present danger that the program may become involved in some of the well-intentioned but over-zealous public relations so typical of the secondary school music program. A plan to "sell" the elementary music program by having the elementary choir sing before every civic luncheon club in the community is a travesty on effective interpretation.

In this area, the specialist requires some professional guidelines, frequent conferences with her principal, and a reasonable amount of common sense. It is basic for the specialist to understand clearly that no plans for any type of public performance within or away from the school should be made without a prior clearance with the principal.

Summary

First, the broad aims of general supervision were considered. They include: (1) the improvement of learning, (2) providing effective educational leadership, (3) establishing warm, friendly working relationships, (4) helping teachers gain greater competencies, (5) evaluating the program, and (6) interpreting the program.

These aims are parallel to those of the elementary music consultant although in some ways the nature of the consultant's job requires different working procedures. The specific aims of elementary music supervision are: (1) to encourage every teacher to include music in the daily program, (2) to improve the music teaching skills of elementary teachers, (3) to help clarify the shared responsibilities of teacher, consultant, and principal, (4) to develop a balanced, coordinated program, (5) to be aware of how music can enrich other learnings, and (6) to interpret the goals and values of the elementary music program.

Questions for Discussion

1. In what ways does the elementary music consultant function like a general supervisor of instruction? In what ways is the consultant's work quite different?

2. What is the basic objective of both general supervision and music supervision?

3. Does the music consultant exert as much official leadership as the general supervisor?

4. What is meant by the term "emergent leadership"?

5. What is meant by the term "recognized leadership"?

6. Discuss this statement: "The special supervisor's participation must convince others that his knowledge is a tool at their service rather than a club to force conformity."

7. Identify several specific aims of elementary music supervision.

8. How would a music teacher approach the introduction of percussive instruments in a primary classroom? How would a music consultant handle the same situation?

9. What would you do if you were employed as a music consultant and you discovered that elementary teachers were accustomed to leaving the room during the consultant's visit?

10. What are some ways that the music specialist can interpret the program of music education to parents, patrons, and the community?

Part Two

The Elementary

Music Consultant

5

How Does the Elementary
Music Consultant Work?

Although the elementary music consultant works in many ways, her day-by-day activities fall into three major categories: (1) working with the elementary teacher and her children in the classroom, (2) working with teacher in-service groups, and (3) conferring with teachers and principals. There are other services she performs but these are her major functions.

Classroom Visits

Most of the work of the elementary music consultant is done through classroom visits. The term "visit" is hardly precise, since a social situation is implied. The word "visitation" is unsatisfactory since it carries with it the idea of official inspection or, perhaps, of something calamitous. Perhaps "service" would be a more appropriate designation. However, the word "visit" is so widely accepted in the literature of supervision that it will be used here to refer to the periodic services provided by the music consultant in the elementary classroom.

1. Scheduled visits. Most of the visits of the elementary music consultant are made on a scheduled basis; that is, the elementary teacher knows the arrival time of the consultant in her classroom. In conducting scheduled visits, the consultant must bear in mind that her role is that of a consulting, helping teacher. There are several practical reasons why it is necessary for her to become directly involved in the teaching-learning situation.

In the literature of supervision, there are many admonitions for the general supervisor to stay out of the teaching situation as much as possible. He is cautioned to enter the room unobtrusively, to take part in class activities only when requested to do so, and to leave quietly at the end of his observation.

Observation is an important technique of supervision. The elementary music consultant is very happy indeed when circumstances enable her to observe the elementary teacher. Such a situation is possible where the consultant knows the teacher very well, where good personal relations exist, and where the elementary teacher has a positive attitude toward music and her ability to teach it. But in elementary music supervision, observation of teaching by the consultant is likely to be the exception rather than the rule. Most teachers do not feel secure enough to teach music while the consultant observes.

There are a number of reasons why the elementary music consultant needs to handle classroom visits in a somewhat different manner than the general supervisor.

Music supervisors came on the educational scene late in the nineteenth century as "expert" teachers to handle one aspect of the elementary curriculum. Teachers wanted help with such "new" subjects as music, art, penmanship, and physical education. These expert teachers or supervisors were expected to take the initiative in teaching. This expectancy for the specialist to "take charge" persists today.

However, this expectancy does not give the elementary music consultant the right to use an authoritative approach. While it is true that earlier supervisors at times set themselves up as inspectors and judges, we know from current research that supervision is most effective when approached as a cooperative enterprise. The elementary music consultant offers help and guidance to the classroom teacher but not to the extent of dictating how she should teach.

Despite improvements that have been made in the pre-service training of elementary teachers, it is still common for many teachers to feel inadequate about teaching music. Actually, the reason for specialist supervision in the elementary school is that teachers have consistently demanded help in the areas of art, physical education, and music. One classroom teacher has put it this way:

> As a third grade teacher and also from a parent point-of-view, I sincerely hope the specialists are here to stay, not least the music specialist.
>
> I feel sure that if a survey were taken of all the classroom elementary teachers in just one school district, a high percentage would

admit insecurity in teaching music—more so than in any other area of learning.[1]

Elementary teachers would be most disappointed if the elementary consultant in music would do no more than observe and offer generalized suggestions. Elementary teachers want specific suggestions and specific help.

It is important that the consultant realize that the elementary teacher has much to offer. In a revealing report of a joint project of music education and elementary education majors at New York University, this interesting conclusion was drawn:

> It was assumed from the start that the music specialist would be the one to impart knowledge and aid in developing the skills of the classroom teacher, but, lo and behold, as the project progressed, it was discovered that the future classroom teacher has as much to offer as the music major. The classroom teacher's knowledge of subject matter at various grade levels, of the growth and physical development of the child, and of classroom procedure soon placed the two participating groups on a relatively equal basis.[2]

The primary objective of classroom visits by the consultant should not be to serve in a tutorial capacity: to teach new songs, dances, and other activities with the idea of coming back in a week to see how well the material has been taught; the presentation of new material will be one phase of classroom visitation, but the teacher-consultant relationship must go much further if the music program is to flourish.

Just what does the elementary music consultant do?

Miss Carol Jones visits Miss Shirley Wells' third-grade class. Miss Wells is interested in learning how to use the autoharp for simple accompaniments. Miss Jones, rather than pointing out to Miss Wells that there are other activities that might take precedence, seizes on this evidenced interest as an entree in working with Miss Wells.

There are several ways that Miss Jones may proceed. She may "take over" entirely and do all or nearly all of the teaching herself. This may be justifiable when there is no other way to get the job done. However, in working with the autoharp in Miss Wells' classroom, Miss Jones knows that this is not necessary. It is much more desirable for Miss Wells to be drawn into the learning process so that she learns *with the children*.

At every step of the way, Miss Jones' continuing aim is to make elementary teachers *as musically independent as possible*. If Miss Wells develops some rudimentary skill in playing the autoharp she has something on which Miss Jones can build. Eventually, Miss Wells will be able to carry on this

[1] Esther Stalsbroten, "Can We Afford the Music Specialist?" *Oregon Music Educator,* May–June, 1962, p. 9.
[2] Solveig D. Preus, "Coordination Is the Key." *Music Educators Journal,* Washington, D. C., January, 1962, p. 86.

phase of her work without help. In fact, in time, she will be able to do much more with the autoharp in her class than Miss Jones could ever hope to accomplish in the course of her weekly visits.

Mrs. Susan Crandall, the fourth-grade teacher, is well prepared and vitally interested in teaching music. She looks on Miss Jones as a consultant and a resource person. She needs help on materials and an occasional word of encouragement but, for the most part, she is able to teach on her own.

By way of contrast, Miss Mary Armstrong, the fifth-grade teacher, would be very happy if she were relieved of all responsibility to teach music. She sees little reason for taking time for music; in fact, she is quite outspoken in stating that the music period could be given over to more important matters. If it were not for Mr. Hawkins' insistence as her supervising principal that she remain in the room during Miss Jones' visits, she would leave "for a well deserved rest."

In this fifth-grade class, Miss Jones accepts the reality that she will need to do all or nearly all of the music teaching herself. She recognizes that these ten-year-olds will have extremely limited experiences in music unless she provides them. However, with Mr. Hawkins' help and support, she will persist in seeking every opportunity to draw Miss Armstrong into music activities. For example, if Miss Armstrong indicates a willingness to play a recording that Miss Jones has already presented to the children during her supervisory visit, Miss Jones considers this a significant accomplishment.

Mrs. Edith McElroy, who now teaches sixth grade, is a former music specialist who decided to return to college to qualify for elementary certification. She is able to do her music work, including the teaching of notation and part-singing, on an independent basis. Miss Jones' visits to Mrs. McElroy's classroom are almost entirely for observation purposes. With Mrs. McElroy's understanding and approval, Miss Jones does not visit her every time she is in the school, but devotes her time to other classes where her services are urgently needed.

Although both extremes have been exemplified (the resistant or musically timid teacher such as Miss Armstrong and the musically independent teacher such as Mrs. McElroy), most teachers fall in Miss Wells' category. Miss Wells is willing to make an effort to teach music but she needs considerable help, guidance, and direction. She is willing to offer suggestions to Miss Jones about how she would like to use music in her room but she is heavily dependent on her for materials and procedures. Most elementary teachers *want* to teach music if given the help that will make it possible for them to do so.

Although there is no formula for planning a "perfect" supervisory visit, Miss Jones attempts, whenever possible, to provide for the following:

(A) During the early part of her visit, she finds it advisable to sing a familiar, appealing song or to arrange for some other activity that establishes immediate rapport. A well-known "greeting song" accomplishes this purpose very well in the primary grades. The singing of a patriotic song might perform the same function in the intermediate grades.

(B) Most of her twenty- or thirty-minute visit is given over to a new experience or an extension of an earlier experience. The presentation of a new song, a new recording, a modified way of playing the autoharp, and a new square dance are typical examples. It is for this part of her visit that Miss Jones expects help from the teacher for re-enforcement during the following week. In practice, Miss Jones generally plans for this learning experience although she makes very clear that she is open to suggestions or requests from the elementary teacher.

(C) Miss Jones makes a deliberate attempt to complete her visit on a positive, successful note. The planned learning experience may either provide its own logical ending or Miss Jones may ask the children to do a familiar dance or sing a favorite song to complete her visit.

Reduced to its simplest terms, a well-planned supervisory visit, like a well-written song or poem or novel, has a beginning, a middle, and an end. Planning must be flexible and the consultant must be willing to adapt to the responses of children and teacher, but, first of all, there *must be a plan.* In addition, it is important that she notes how much of the plan was actually implemented and that she makes some evaluation for future reference. The lame opening used by too many specialists, "Well, boys and girls, what did we do last week?" is hardly impressive to teacher or students.

Although the elementary music consultant may feel that her services are needed to a greater extent in the upper elementary grades, she should not leave primary teachers to their own resources. At a meeting of specialists in art, music, and physical education held in conjunction with teachers, supervisors, and administrators, "conferees disapproved of confining the services of special teachers to the upper grades. Primary grades, too, they said, need enrichment of their curriculum, and for some reasons need it particularly."[3]

We have indicated in a number of ways that the attitude or point-of-view of the elementary teacher is of prime importance. The attitude or point-of-view of the specialist is also a very large factor in conducting successful classroom visits. Myers points out one significant aspect of the problem when she says, "The product of the music school needs some *leavening* experiences that will transform his respect, his regard, and his reverence for his subject-matter into the more normal attitude of the nonspecialist."[4]

The danger for the elementary music specialist is that she may be able to see nothing but her special subject area.

2. On-call visits. An on-call visit is the kind of service that the con-

[3] Ralph G. Beelke and Elsa Schneider, "Role of the Special Teacher," *School Life,* March 1957, Vol. 39, No. 6 (Washington, D. C.: U. S. Department of Health, Education and Welfare), p. 11.

[4] Louise Kifer Myers, *Teaching Children Music in the Elementary School,* 3rd ed. (Englewood Cliffs, N. J.: Prentice-Hall, Inc., 1961), p. 237.

sultant welcomes most. It means that she is being called in to work on a specific problem at the request of the teacher.

Carol Jones, invited to Mrs. Swanson's second grade during her "on-call hour," is alerted by Mr. Hawkins that Mrs. Swanson is interested in using the new recordings that have just been purchased for the primary grades. Miss Jones is able to do a great deal in a comparatively short time because the teacher is interested in the recordings and is anxious to put them to use.

One of the cardinal rules of elementary music supervision is *never* to ignore a direct request from a teacher no matter how trivial or insignificant it may appear to be. There is nothing more devastating to morale than for a teacher to request help without action of any kind being taken; at the very least, the consultant should indicate to the teacher that the sought-for material is not available or that the requested activity is inappropriate. To simply pigeonhole a request for help will discourage a teacher from making future requests.

Should the elementary music consultant work "on schedule" or "on call"? Obviously, she must be prepared to work both ways.

Even if the consultant is employed to work entirely "on call," which rarely happens, many teachers who need help most may not request it. The music consultant has the responsibility not only to serve in a consultative capacity but also to provide strong educational leadership in developing a comprehensive elementary music program. She cannot sit by as an interested spectator who enters into the program only when invited to do so.

In practical terms, the elementary music consultant will spend a greater part of her time on scheduled visits. If one hour of her working day can be set aside for "on-call" requests in each school that she serves, Miss Jones considers herself very fortunate indeed. Of course, it is important that she have good communication with her principal in planning her working schedule and in carrying it out. It is quite possible for some project (a presentation of an operetta by Mrs. Crandall's fourth-grade class, for example) to be considered so important that the scheduled visits may be temporarily adjusted to provide more time for this "on-call" service. In making adjustments in her supervisory schedule, Miss Jones must have the guidance and support of her principal.

3. *Unscheduled visits.* There probably will not be many opportunities for unscheduled visits in the course of the elementary music consultant's day. They are possible only when good rapport has been established between teacher and consultant, where there is a mutual feeling of trust and respect, and where the consultant has free time. When a teacher tells Miss Jones, "Please stop by my room anytime that you have a few extra minutes, I shall always be happy to see you come," she can feel quite sure that she has been accepted as a true resource helper. Although unscheduled visits will occupy

only a small part of Miss Jones' day, they represent unique opportunities for professional growth.

In-Service Groups

One way of working with teachers that has not been extensively developed in elementary music supervision is in-service programs. The classroom visit is, and will continue to be, the basic function of the music consultant. However, along with supervision on a person-to-person basis, there is a need for teachers to meet and work together in group situations. Some achievements may be made through the group process that are difficult or impossible to accomplish in classroom visits.

Although it is possible to organize study groups in many ways, there is overwhelming evidence to indicate that the building faculty group should be the basic unit in a program of in-service education. There may also be an occasional need to organize interschool groups (such as all first grade teachers) but, by and large, the building group should serve as the focal point for in-service work in the elementary school.

How does one go about organizing in-service groups?

It should be quite clear that just because the music consultant would like to organize an in-service group, this does not mean that teachers will jump at the opportunity. The group must work on problems they consider to be timely and important. Teachers must be ready to work because they are interested, not because someone else is interested.

It is certainly easier to organize faculty studies when one works in a school system committed to the concept of faculty improvement through group study. If so, it is logical to assume that, along with efforts made to improve other instructional areas, appropriate planning will also be provided for music and the arts.

If there is no system-wide organization for in-service work, the problem is more difficult. In any case, the elementary music consultant will find it advisable to begin with the principal. If he is interested, and if he thinks his faculty may be interested, there is reason to believe that hope may become reality. Although it is desirable that the entire faculty participate, it is not essential. If the principal agrees to organize an in-service group on a voluntary basis, the consultant should welcome the opportunity to begin this way.

A word of caution: The elementary music consultant should not be too surprised if it takes some time to develop faculty readiness to participate in in-service work. It may take even the most resourceful consultant several years to bring about the organization of a working faculty group.

Once a principal and faculty have indicated that they are willing to work on an experimental basis to improve the music education program, how do we proceed?

There are many possible ways of working. As a basic premise, remember that it is important to discover the interests and concerns of the group. If Miss Carol Jones is excited about using a class-piano approach with the Broadmoor Elementary School faculty, but discovers that the majority of the teachers are much more interested in improving the listening program, she would be most unwise to insist on the class-piano idea.

A fundamental precept of group work is that it be *problem-centered*. The problem to be worked on must be of interest to all, it must be clearly defined, and it must be sufficiently limited so that the chance for a successful completion in the time available is assured.

Several generalizations are in order concerning in-service work:

(A) Most teachers prefer a *doing* activity; that is, actually making music rather than talking about it. Teachers are looking for specific things they can use in their classroom tomorrow. They become impatient with an in-service meeting where the values of music education in the elementary school are discussed remotely or abstractly.

Not only is there a need to do things, but there is a far greater chance of success if the activities are quite sharply focused. For example, one group might be interested in a more functional use of recordings. Another group may want to consider the use of simple instruments in the classroom. Still another may want to concentrate on singing games and folk dances. A loosely organized approach can work in some situations but the prospects of success are much greater if there is a specific purpose and a continuing interest that makes the participants feel that they have attained concrete goals after the meetings are completed.

(B) Although it is important to teach songs, dances, rhythms, etc., in in-service groups, there should be an even more important objective. Too often in-service work is a case of "filling up the hopper" with assorted ideas and materials. Although this is of some value, it is a limited concept. In in-service study, everything possible should be done to promote the musical growth of the participants and to have them achieve, if only in a very small way, some measure of musical independence.

Carol Jones was successful in organizing one group that used class piano as a point of departure. Her objective was to teach the group members enough piano so that they could play a single line melody from their basic music books and perform simple I, IV, and V chord accompaniments. The objectives were modest in terms of pianistic ability but this limited proficiency gave teachers a valuable working tool.

Mrs. Beth Swanson, for example, is now able to "pick out" a new Halloween song for her boys and girls from the second-grade book without help. She would have strong reservations about playing the piano at an assembly program but she has developed enough skill to learn new songs independently.

(C) Although it is expected that the elementary music consultant will take a positive leadership role, she should not dominate the group in an autocratic way. She encourages teachers to take over discussions and presentations and she strongly supports signs of emergent leadership. In short, like the general supervisor, she should consider group work a democratic process.

(D) There are many possible procedures in conducting in-service groups. For example, the professional in-service meetings in the Central City Schools are set up on an every-other-week basis, a total of about fifteen meetings during the year. Although this may seem to be a limited amount of time, much can be accomplished.

Of course, Miss Carol Jones must be flexible in adjusting her schedule to the wishes of the group. If one faculty elects to meet weekly while another faculty chooses to meet only once a month, she should be willing to meet on their terms. Generally, meetings will be held after the school day is completed. The details of meeting times are properly the province of the principal and his faculty working within general conditions set by the central office.

In planning for in-service meetings, the elementary consultant realizes:

that the problem being considered must be taken into account in establishing the size of the group. A class-piano group of eight might be ideal. However, the consultant could present a recently adopted music series to thirty teachers without difficulty.

that a period of one hour or one-and-one-half hours is generally needed for a satisfactory session.

that the group process must be democratic, flexible, informal, and creative with a provision for emergent leadership.

that the problem must be appropriate, stimulating, and challenging. It should be agreed upon before the group begins to function.

that a comfortable atmosphere is conducive to a successful group meeting. An attractive room, a circle of chairs in a conversational setting, and a cup of coffee all contribute in a positive way.

that bringing people together makes possible a "group mind" that may be more productive than isolated, individual thinking.

that due consideration should be given to group metabolism. Signs of fatigue should be noted: teachers have put in a full day! Change of pace is just as necessary in planning for in-service groups as for classroom teaching.

Faculty meetings, especially if they are called for instructional purposes rather than for administrative routine, offer opportunities for the consultant to work with the total faculty when invited to do so. There is not as much chance for extensive participation as in an organized study group, but some good may be accomplished.

It is encouraging to note that more and more faculty meetings are concerned with problems of instruction as principals recognize that their responsibility is at least as great for the supervision of instruction as for administration in their schools.

Conferences

Ideally, the consultant would welcome the opportunity to have a discussion with the elementary teacher after each visit. In practice, this frequently takes the form of a few comments made as the consultant is ready to leave the classroom. This will often be the only person-to-person discussion between consultant and teacher.

Although there are specific suggestions and instructions that may be handled in this manner, there will be times when the consultant needs a conference to discuss the program at length, where mutual evaluations can be made, and where appropriate "next steps" can be agreed on by teacher and consultant.

If a problem exists that requires extended discussion, the elementary music consultant needs an opportunity to talk with the teacher when the children are not present. As a word of advice, the teacher is always more comfortable when the conference is held in her own classroom. It is important for the consultant to bear in mind that a conference has as its central purpose the improvement of musical offerings and that it is not to be regarded primarily as a critique of the teacher's shortcomings. A successful conference produces cooperative planning for more effective teaching. It should not be held for the purpose of imposing the consultant's plan of action on the classroom teacher.

Conferences may be initiated by the consultant or the teacher, and it is also hoped that the principal will involve himself in requesting and arranging them. Efforts should be made to hold *scheduled* conferences as often as practicable. At times, the impromptu or unplanned conference may uncover concerns of significance.

Additional Services

The elementary consultant, in addition to making service visits to the classroom, conducting in-service meetings, and holding conferences, will also be called on for other types of resource help. Such requests as assistance on materials, arranging for intervisitation for elementary teachers, and acting as a liaison person for community music activities are all a part of the job. In attempting to meet these requests for additional services, the constant criterion should be to determine to what extent they contribute to improved instruction in the classroom.

To function as a resource person, the elementary music consultant must be flexible and versatile. She must keep up-to-date on the wealth of new materials on elementary music education that are published each year. She must see to it that adequate supplies and materials are provided to classroom teachers. She must be familiar not only with trends and issues in music education but in the broader field of elementary education as well.

One of the most common requests for additional service comes in the form of preparing public performances. Most often this will be an activity such as developing an elementary chorus, staging an operetta, presenting a rhythm band for the P.T.A., or accompanying a show for the annual carnival night.

In the case of the elementary chorus, there is certainly merit in giving interested youngsters in the upper elementary grades an opportunity to prepare songs that go beyond the confines of classroom performance. To sing a group of well prepared songs with an adequate accompaniment in a performance situation is a rewarding experience for any child.

The desirable activity becomes questionable when the group becomes a highly selective organization that causes "in" and "out" musical segregation in the upper elementary grades. The *school chorus,* organized on the basis of interest rather than special talent, is a much sounder approach than the overly-selective elementary choir.

Even more questionable is the practice followed in some schools of permitting the elementary choir to take the place of the classroom program in the fifth and sixth grade. Under this procedure, youngsters elect to sing in the chorus or they receive no music instruction.

A guiding precept for elementary supervision should be to always give primary emphasis to the *basic classroom program.* This should be sacrosanct. No other musical activity in the elementary school, including instruction in instrumental music, should be given precedence.

The danger of permitting undue pressure for public performance to become so strong at the secondary level that it actually impairs the fundamental purpose of music education is too familiar to review at this point. The elementary music program is the only phase of music education that has a good chance of reaching *all* boys and girls. It is a phase of the program where the emphasis is placed squarely on what music means to the individual. The elementary music specialist must see to it that *the basic classroom program is always given primary consideration.*

Summary

We have pointed out that the work of the elementary music consultant falls into three major categories: (1) classroom visits, (2) in-service work, and (3) conferences.

In the classroom visitation program, the elementary music consultant does less observing than the general supervisor and becomes more directly involved in the teaching process. However, she must function democratically if the cooperative approach is to be successful.

Whenever possible, the consultant works to make the classroom teacher increasingly independent. The specialist brings new ideas, new materials, and new procedures into the classroom. However, she should be as concerned in working *with the teacher* as she is in working with children.

"On-call" requests are particularly welcome since they give the consultant an opportunity to work on a specific problem that has been identified by the teacher. The consultant never ignores this type of request for assistance.

In-service group work has not been used in elementary music supervision as extensively as it should be. It offers great possibilities for bringing about improvement in the instructional program. The consultant may need to work for a considerable time in organizing an in-service group. The logical person with whom to begin is the principal. The building faculty group is the basic unit for in-service work. It is important that the group be problem-centered.

Conferences may be initiated by the teacher, the consultant, or the principal. They may range from a few words spoken at the end of a classroom visit to a relaxed, unhurried, professional discussion. Some problems are best discussed when the children are not present. The unplanned conference, too, may be of great value.

Many additional requests for services are made of the elementary music consultant. As a rule-of-thumb, no additional service or activity should be encouraged if it functions at the expense of the basic classroom music program.

Questions for Discussion

1. Do you think that it is easier to serve as a music teacher or as a music consultant? Give reasons for your answer.
2. React to this statement: "The music consultant must know the individual elementary teachers she serves as well as a teacher knows her children."
3. What are some valid criteria in evaluating a classroom visit of the music consultant?
4. How does the consultant plan for a classroom visit?
5. Which teachers require more specialist help, primary teachers or upper grade teachers? Why?
6. What is meant by an "on call" visit? Give several illustrations.
7. Why is it so important that the elementary music consultant never ignore a direct request for assistance from the elementary teacher?
8. What are some things that may be accomplished in in-service study groups that are difficult or impossible to achieve in classroom visits?
9. What are some factors to consider in planning for in-service groups?
10. List several objectives of teacher-consultant conferences.

6

Responsibilities of
Elementary Music Supervision

The elementary music consultant, particularly if she works in a situation where she serves several schools, may be uncertain as to her responsibilities and the persons to whom she is responsible. And, conversely, she may wonder what responsibilities other members of the educational team have to her as a music consultant.

A teacher who is a member of a school faculty with a definite classroom assignment has clearly drawn responsibilities. Miss Carol Jones does not have a classroom assignment nor is she considered to be a member of the central office supervisory staff. She often wonders just where her responsibilities as a music consultant begin and end.

Responsibilities to Children in the Classroom

The basic responsibility that the teacher, specialist, supervisor, and administrator has to the child in the classroom is so obvious that it seems unnecessary to mention it at all. Without question, the growth of boys and girls in musical responsiveness is the *primary* responsibility of the elementary music specialist.

This responsibility is as fundamental as it is obvious. It is the center of gravity for the elementary music specialist's work, it is the reference point for the formulation of her working philosophy, it is the basis for her day-by-day planning.

The elementary music consultant is the person most directly responsible for the improvement of music instruction in the elementary school. She visits classrooms, conducts in-service meetings, and holds conferences. She is concerned with such matters as the quality and quantity of books, recordings, record players, and other instructional material. All of these responsibilities are directly related to the improvement of musical experiences for boys and girls.

In any consultant-supervisory work, there will be stresses and pulls in responsibilities. At times there may be outright conflicts.

For example, Mr. Hawkins, the principal of Broadmoor Elementary School, has had a conference with the mother of a child who sings in the school chorus. She has suggested that Miss Jones concentrate her energies for the next two months on preparing the group for the annual district music festival competition. Mr. Hawkins explained to the mother that Miss Jones could do so only at the expense of the basic classroom program. The mother feels that the rating that the chorus will receive is of such importance to the school and the community that Miss Jones should de-emphasize the classroom work if necessary.

Both Mr. Hawkins and Miss Jones, after discussing the situation, realize that this would be an opportunity for the school to obtain recognition for the quality of the work that the choir is doing. They also recognize that the choir's rating would be interpreted by many as an indication of the quality of the entire school music program.

However, both Mr. Hawkins and Miss Jones agree that the consultant's major responsibility is to classroom instruction. The choir continues to meet on its regular schedule. The basic classroom program continues to receive its primary emphasis. In this potential conflict of responsibilities for both principal and consultant, the decision is made in terms of the greatest good for all concerned.

Responsibilities to Professional Personnel

1. Responsibility to elementary teachers. Like her responsibility to children, the music consultant's responsibility to the elementary teacher is obvious. If it were not for this responsibility, Miss Jones would not have a position at all. It is her job to guide, assist, and support elementary teachers in their efforts to provide vital, meaningful experiences in music for children.

Often the beginning elementary music consultant is perplexed by her shared responsibility with the elementary teacher. If Miss Mary Armstrong, the fifth-grade teacher, asks for help with a musical activity that Miss Jones feels is questionable, must she acquiesce? And if Miss Jones suggests a music activity only to discover that Miss Armstrong strongly diapproves, what next steps should Miss Jones take? Should not Mr. Hawkins require Miss Armstrong to do what the consultant recommends?

The consultant-teacher relationship operates best without sharply delineated, authoritative lines. The elementary music consultant's suggestions are taken not because teachers *must* take them but because they *want* to take them. Music supervision becomes effective when it is concerned more with human factors and less with rules and regulations.

The experienced elementary music consultant knows very well that music taught by a teacher coerced into doing so against her will is likely to be most unrewarding. Music is so loaded with affective, emotional elements that the attitude of the teacher, as much as any other factor, is responsible for the success or failure of the classroom musical experiences.

2. Responsibility to principals. The music educator needs to remember that the principal is the *supervisor* of his building as well as its *administrator*. He is as responsible for the music program as he is for language arts, mathematics, and science. The principal feels, and rightfully so, that the principles of good teaching apply in music education as they do in other fields. He considers himself in a position to evaluate the effectiveness of instruction in music even though his formal musical training may be limited.

However, it must also be pointed out that principals, like many teachers, feel much more inadequate about music education than they do other subject areas. They need and welcome help and guidance from the specialist. Emphasizing this fact but also reminding us of the principal's ultimate responsibility Wiles has this to say, "Supervisors, general and special, are available as consultants and helpers, but they cannot direct the work of individual teachers in a manner contrary to the wishes of the principal. If they do, the principal cannot be held responsible for the program in his building."[1]

The elementary music consultant must realize that the professional supervisor to whom she is directly responsible is *the principal* of the schools she serves. This is true even though there may be an overall supervisor or director of music for the entire school system.

Ideas as to scheduling, ways of working, and plans for performance are often initiated by the music consultant, but no instructional endeavor can operate independently of the total program. The music consultant, after thoroughly discussing a problem with her principal, must be as willing to accept his final decision as would any other teacher on his faculty. The final decision on a question regarding the curriculum is the prerogative of the principal because the final responsibility is also his.

[1] Kimball Wiles, *Supervision for Better Schools,* 2nd ed. (Englewood Cliffs, N. J.: Prentice-Hall, Inc., 1955), p. 152.

Miss Carol Jones does not encourage the professional staff or lay people to think of the music program in a particular school as *her* program. She makes clear that it is the program of the school and its faculty under the instructional supervision of the principal.

Does the principal have a responsibility to the elementary music consultant?

Most assuredly he does. If there is any predominant criticism elementary music consultants have about their work it is that administrators and, specifically, principals do not indicate that they feel as strong a responsibility for music as they do other subject areas.

"How can we get the principal to see that music has an important function as a discipline in its own right?" is a question often raised in discussion groups of elementary music specialists. "If he were concerned or even aware of what we are trying to do, my job would be much easier and much more satisfying."

Too often elementary music specialists feel that principals and administrators are not as interested in music education as they are in other curriculum areas. There is a need for mutual understanding and a realization that all concerned have a common goal: the improvement of instruction in the classroom.

There will be conflicts when the elementary music specialist attempts to develop and expand *her* program without so much as a by-your-leave from the principal. One of the best starting points for improving the music program is a series of professional conferences between the principal and his music consultant. In these conferences, responsibilities should be defined and steps for curriculum improvement outlined.

3. Responsibility to the music staff. In music education in the public schools there are three major classifications or sub-groups: (1) instrumental music teachers, (2) secondary vocal music teachers, and (3) elementary music specialists. Of these, the sub-group that is least active in professional matters, the least vocal in indicating its needs, is the elementary music specialists. Yet many educators, including instrumental music teachers and secondary vocal music teachers, agree that the elementary music specialist can make as great an impact on the minds and hearts of children as any other music educator in the public schools.

The elementary music specialist has a very real responsibility to work actively with other members of the music staff. If Roy Peters, the high school bandsman, indicates an interest in Miss Jones' teaching, she should also recognize that she might work more effectively by seeing her contributions in the perspective of Mr. Peters' responsibility.

Just as the elementary music program cannot develop outside the confines of the general classroom program, the elementary music program cannot develop without a concern for and an understanding of the total music curriculum. Periodic meetings of the total music staff are indispensable if professional growth is to occur within the system. Elementary music special-ists should welcome such opportunities and should participate in them en-thusiastically.

However, a word of caution is in order. Working cooperatively with secondary teachers does *not* mean that the elementary music specialist should revamp her work to "prepare" boys and girls for high school.

Elementary music specialists, by and large, are much more sensitive to the developmental abilities and limitations of children at varying maturity levels than their secondary school colleagues. They should take a firm stand on procedures and objectives that are based on findings of developmental psychology.

Secondly, music teachers in the secondary school are apt to forget the fact that the elementary music specialist works with *all* boys and girls and not only with the especially interested students that elect music in high school. What is proposed as satisfactory criteria for students entering the cadet band may or may not be valid criteria for all children in the elementary music progam.

4. Responsibility to the supervisor of music. As the elementary music specialist is responsible to the principal as her supervisor in the operational phase of the program, the elementary music specialist is responsible to the supervisor of music in his role as the coordinating force and recognized leader in the field of music education. It is important for the elementary music specialists to keep him informed not only of problems but also of practices. She should make known her suggestions for improving supervisory services and submit her requests to him for instructional materials. It is strongly rec-ommended that the elementary music specialist and the supervisor of music meet together regularly to facilitate exchange of information, to evaluate, and to plan for continued improvement.

The supervisor of music, of course, can be of great help to the elemen-tary music specialist. James Hughes, Supervisor of Music in the Central City Schools, serves as a spokesman for Miss Carol Jones at the central office level. He represents her needs as to schedule, plans for curriculum develop-ment, and materials. He can speak to her principals on a peer relationship basis. He helps organize such projects as in-service group meetings. It will be his normal responsibility to serve as administrator to Miss Jones in order-ing supplies, providing instructional materials, maintaining equipment, and related functions.

5. Responsibility to supervisors and administrators. The elementary music specialist has the same professional responsibility to the director of curriculum and the superintendent as any other teacher on the professional staff. The general expectations that the administrator has for all teachers apply to the elementary music specialist including teaching hours, participa-tion in workshops, attendance at meetings, and general professional de-portment.

The elementary music specialist does both herself and her profession a disservice when she assumes that as a specialist she is entitled to special treatment and to special privileges. When extra consideration is given to Miss Jones, such as allowing her to have a flexible visitation schedule, she must not abuse the privilege.

It is difficult for the specialist to realize that the very broad responsibilities that the superintendent and other administrative officers have may not always make it possible for them to bring about immediate adjustments in the elementary music program—even if they would like to do so. There may be needs even more pressing than those of the elementary music specialist.

The specialist who seeks an appointment with an administrative officer, not to ask for something, but to inform him as to the status and progress of a program will have a somewhat surprised and pleased listener. To seek out an administrator only when one wants something is poor practice. The specialist has a responsibility to keep the administrator informed and to help him evaluate the music offerings as a part of the total educational program.

Finally, Miss Carol Jones should bear in mind that the reason that the administration and board of education have employed her as a music consultant is because the instructional staff cannot carry on a desired program without her services. In a very real sense, Mr. R. L. Simmons, Superintendent of Central City Schools, has delegated a part of his responsibility for supervision of instruction to Miss Jones as an especially qualified assistant. Miss Jones, then, is responsible to Mr. Simmons for the discharge of this delegated responsibility. If the music education program in a system is unsatisfactory to many patrons, the person who is held ultimately responsible by the board of education is the superintendent.

Responsibilities to the Community

1. Responsibility to board members. Like all teachers, supervisors, and administrators, the elementary music specialist is a professional employee appointed by the superintendent and approved by members of the school board or board of education. In the Central City Schools the board of education holds the Superintendent, Mr. R. L. Simmons, responsible for the professional qualifications of his staff as well as for the scope and quality of the program of education.

Mr. Simmons requires the services of many teachers, principals, and supervisors to help him discharge his responsibility. Miss Carol Jones, as we have indicated, is employed to assist Mr. Simmons with his instructional responsibility as it relates to the area of elementary music education.

As a professional employee, Miss Jones must remember that her problems and needs are the province of her principal, her supervisors, and the superintendent. To approach individual board members for a quick solution of an administrative problem is extremely unprofessional and is dangerous not only to herself but to every other professional employee in the system.

Most beginning teachers are not aware of the fact that the individual board member has no direct authority except when meeting with the full board. As Davies and Hosler explain:

> In an official meeting the board has far-reaching authority. But board members separately, outside of an official meeting, have no legal right or power to act for the schools. The law gives authority only to the board as a whole. A few minor exceptions occur, such as limited specific duties delegated by law to the board president, secretary, and treasurer.[2]

Therefore, the practice of the music specialist, or any other professional employee, of approaching individual board members on matters of an administrative or supervisory nature is to be strongly discouraged. If Miss Jones does so, she circumvents principals, supervisors, and the superintendent himself in the discharge of their legal responsibilities. Board members are entrusted with the broad responsibility of policy making. The function of the school board is primarily *legislative*. The *executive* function, of working out the details of how policies are to be carried out, is the responsibility of the superintendent and his professional staff.

2. Responsibility to the music education profession. The elementary music specialist, like any teacher in music education, has definite responsibilities to the *professional community* of which she is a member. She must look beyond the problems of her own particular assignment and see her job in the setting of a larger body of professional workers in her area, in her state, and across the nation.

It should be quite clear that the present status of music education represents the cumulative and cooperative efforts of thousands upon thousands of teachers who have devoted their energies to bringing music education to the high level that distinguishes it today. All of us are willing to accept privileges won by our predecessors. All of us should be willing, too, to accept the responsibility for continuing our professional advancement.

The elementary music specialist must not only be willing but she should be eager to work on study groups or committees within the school system. She should be willing to extend her services to regional groups when she is invited to do so. The development of curriculum guides is impossible without the unselfish contributions of many skilled, experienced practitioners. No professional state music association can exist without the willingness of its members to serve in a wide variety of ways.

In this connection, it must again be pointed out that instrumental

[2] Daniel R. Davies and Fred W. Hosler, *The Challenge of School Board Membership* (New York: Chartwell House, Inc., 1951), p. 11.

music teachers and high school choral directors have gone much further in accepting this kind of professional responsibility than elementary music specialists. The rather limited attention given to the special needs and interests of elementary music supervision at state and regional conventions is indicative of the limited degree of professional responsibility of this kind that has been accepted by elementary music specialists. They must be willing to permit their names to be submitted for office, they must be willing to take on administrative duties within the professional community, and they must be broad enough in their outlook to embrace widespread and far-reaching concerns of music education.

The elementary music specialist represents one of the most important, if not *the* most important, level in music education. However, she has not made her influence felt in professional matters in any way commensurate with the important role she plays.

3. Responsibility to community patrons. The elementary music specialist's responsibility to the community is mainly in terms of interpreting the program to parents and patrons. Miss Jones wants people to hear and see something of the work that is being done in the elementary program. In this process of interpreting, Miss Jones also hopes that there will be possibilities for entertainment. Although the dangers of over-emphasizing the entertainment and under-emphasizing the interpretation are not as great at the elementary as at the secondary level, there is a necessity for keeping things in proper balance.

The most direct interpretation is what students have to say to their parents about their school music experiences. Parents will appraise the merits of the program on this basis more than they will in any other way. Miss Jones finds that it is helpful to stop and summarize with her boys and girls just what it is that they are accomplishing. Students should be able to identify learnings and the values of these learnings. When parents ask their children, "What are you doing in music this year?" we should assist them in being able to give articulate, positive responses.

Public appearances of music groups at the elementary level are not as common as at the secondary level but they should be planned just as carefully. People attending an elementary school performance are interested and sympathetic. They expect an acceptable performance but they are not hypercritical. In her planning the elementary music specialist should make sure that programs are not too long. Adult audiences also have interest-span limitations.

There may be special occasions when elementary groups travel away from the school for a public appearance but these should be held to a minimum. Demonstrations within the school at P.T.A. meetings, go-to-school night, and similar functions offer excellent opportunities for the music specialists to interpret the music program. Miss Jones conducts these demonstrations in the regular classroom setting whenever she is able to do so. The demonstrations should be relaxed, informal, and as close to the typical learning situation as possible. Approaching the demonstration on the basis of "an example of what we are doing in our music program" is a sound procedure.

Elementary music specialists, by and large, are not as alert as their secondary school colleagues in informing the community of activities and accomplishments through the media of newspapers, radio, and television. The concert of the high school band is duly reported in the newspaper. The program of the elementary choir is not. Usually the reason is that the high school band director has filed an account of the forthcoming program with the local paper while the elementary music specialist has failed to do so. From the point of view of the city editor, the elementary program has perhaps even greater "human interest" appeal. Ordinarily, he will be happy to provide appropriate space, but he must be given the information.

Radio and television appearances pose many of the same problems as other out-of-school appearances. They must be scheduled carefully and with constant concern that interpreting a program does not also become a process of exploiting children. Television is particularly effective for the presentation of elementary groups since the visual appeal is enormously important in indicating the joy and satisfaction that significant music-making brings to boys and girls.

Summary

The responsibilities of the elementary music consultant are not always as clearly drawn as those of the classroom teacher. She may be uncertain as to many of her professional responsibilities, and she may not be aware of responsibilities that other professional workers have to her.

The consultant's first responsibility is to the children in the classroom. All curriculum decisions should be made on the basis of this primary responsibility.

The consultant's responsibility to elementary teachers is obvious: She is employed because teachers want assistance and guidance in music. The consultant-teacher relationship functions best without authoritative controls. Teachers should want to take suggestions from the consultant rather than being required to take them.

The consultant must bear in mind that the principal is both supervisor of instruction as well as the administrator of his building. He may not feel adequate in the area of music education, but he is prepared to evaluate the effectiveness of music instruction by applying to it the principles of good teaching. The consultant is directly responsible to the school principal.

The principal, too, has a responsibility to the consultant. He indicates his expectancy to teachers that music must be included in the daily program. He is aware of the current status of music instruction and he should support and encourage its further development.

Elementary music specialists should be willing to work on problems of general concern to the total music staff. They need to clarify their goals and objectives with other music teachers and they must see their work in the perspective of the responsibilities of instrumental music teachers and secondary vocal music teachers.

Elementary music specialists are responsible to the supervisor of music in his capacity as the official, recognized leader in music education. They should keep him informed about problems and practices. They look to him for professional guidance in improving their services, in working with individual principals, and in organizing in-service programs. They depend on the supervisor of music for essential, administrative leadership.

The responsibilities of the elementary music specialist to general supervisors and administrators are the same as that of any other teacher on the professional staff. If there is a question as to whom the specialist should see on a professional problem she should first seek the advice of her principal. It is most unprofessional for the specialist to approach individual school board members on administrative matters.

The specialist is responsible to the professional community of which she is a member. She must be willing to look beyond the confines of her own job and see her contributions as they relate to other music educators in her area, the state, and across the country.

In regard to the community, her primary responsibility is in terms of interpreting the program. There are dangers in over-emphasizing entertainment and under-emphasizing interpretation. Public performances must be carefully planned. Efforts should be made to utilize the communications media to help interpret the elementary music program to the community.

Questions for Discussion

1. We have indicated that the elementary teacher is a key figure in the elementary music program. Yet in this chapter we state that the elementary music consultant "is the person most directly responsible for the improvement of music instruction in the elementary school." Is there an inconsistency in these statements?

2. Do you believe it would be wise for the elementary music consultant to have official authority over elementary teachers?

3. What is your reaction to the concept that the principal is the supervisor of music in his building just as he is supervisor of other subject areas?

4. In a possible conflict of responsibilities, to whom is the elementary music consultant directly responsible, the principal or the supervisor of music?

5. What are some of the things elementary music specialists must do in order to earn improved status within the profession?

6. An individual board member is visiting in your school where you are working as an elementary music specialist. He directs you to do something that is contrary to standard policy. What is your professional obligation to him?

7. Discuss this statement: "The superintendent delegates a part of his supervisory responsibility for instruction when he employs an elementary music consultant."

8. In your opinion, is adequate attention given to the special problems of elementary music specialists at state and regional music conventions?

9. What is the way in which most parents judge the quality of a music program?

10. Suggest some guidelines for public performances at the elementary level.

7

Which Musical Learnings
Should Be Emphasized?

It is well accepted that a comprehensive program of elementary music education must include a variety of approaches to musical learning. However, there is not full agreement among music educators concerning the kinds of learnings that should take place. For example, we believe that listening is an important approach to musical understanding. But listening for what? To what kind of music? For what purpose?

The accepted approaches to musical learning—often referred to as activities—include:

Singing
Moving in response to music
Listening
Playing classroom instruments
Creating
Reading music

The first four approaches are universally recognized and are to be found in varying degrees in every classroom with a semblance of a music program. Creating and reading music are not as widely recognized as distinct approaches. Many music educators are of the opinion that creativity is inherent in any music-making and that it cannot be isolated as a separate activity. Others feel that reading music at the elementary level should not be emphasized to the extent that it becomes as important an approach as singing or listening.

Actually, it is dangerous to think of any of the approaches as though they were tightly compartmentalized. Is it possible for one to sing without listening or moving or creating? Can one play an instrument without listening or moving or creating and, perhaps, reading? When we emphasize one approach we are giving it focal interest. No approach can be considered in isolation.

Creativity certainly deserves to be emphasized as a focal interest in a comprehensive program of music education. It is a major approach to musical understanding.

Music reading also deserves major emphasis. In current practice, however, the emphasis that reading should receive is a matter of some controversy. In the 1940's the social-studies orientation for music programs was so very strong that music reading was not only de-emphasized, it was pointedly ignored. The place of music in the curriculum was justified largely on the basis of its enrichment and recreational values. The idea that music in the elementary school was to be taught as a significant learning in its own right was considered to be overly idealistic and quite impractical.

Although we are grateful for the enrichment and recreational values that music has, they are rather shaky pillars on which to build a solid, educational program. Most music educators now hold to the opinion that there is a very great deal about music itself that children should know and experience and appreciate. We should, for example, feel free to sing an expressive art song such as Schubert's "The Linden Tree" even though it may correlate with nothing that is going on in other areas of instruction.

We recognize these following six basic approaches to musical understanding: (1) singing, (2) moving to music, (3) listening, (4) playing instruments, (5) creating, and (6) reading music. They should not be considered as compartmented activities. They should be regarded as *complementary approaches to musical understanding*.

Musical Learnings

Thus far we have discussed either activities or approaches to musical learning. Although activity is a perfectly good word, it does not imply an overriding concern for values, outcomes, or learnings. The fact that twenty minutes of music activity is provided for in the daily classroom schedule guarantees one very little. It is possible to have a listening activity, for example, without learning very much of any value. We should concern ourselves as much with *what* is taught as *how* it is taught.

Is it enough to sing, move, listen, play, create, and read music? Do the activities themselves produce an effective program? Does it make any difference what we sing? When we move to music does it make any difference what kind of music we use?

In the field of elementary music education we have not clearly defined those musical learnings that we hope to achieve. Some of the many reasons for this are: (1) the variables of the job; (2) the too often poorly-defined role of the specialist; (3) the limited pre-service preparation of many elementary teachers; and (4) the apathy on the part of many persons involved.

It is essential for the elementary music specialist to have a clear-cut idea of what musical learnings should be emphasized in the elementary program. She certainly must know what she wants before she can hope to have others cooperate with her in the achievement of her goals. What do we hope to accomplish in the way of musical learnings in a good elementary music program? How do we go about accomplishing them?

First, let us enumerate those broad musical learnings that we believe to be of special appropriateness and significance for the elementary program. They are:

Mood
Tone
Melody
Rhythm
Form
Harmony

In considering these learnings it is important for us to recognize a number of things. First, the learnings are complementary to each other rather than mutually exclusive. Second, the list is not definitive, although it does represent considered thinking as to those that are of prime significance and appropriateness. Third, the approaches made in the elementary school are, of course, an introduction to each of these learnings. Any one of them, even for the professional musician, invites a life-time of study. And last, but by no means least, we must constantly relate desired musical learnings to the developmental abilities of children in the classroom.

Let us examine each of these learnings in turn. As we do so, we shall relate them to the primary grades (kindergarten through grade three) and the intermediate grades (grades four through six).

Mood

In simplest terms, mood is concerned with the way music makes us feel. One of the first ways in which music appeals to us is through feeling. As we sing, play, or listen, some music makes us feel gay and light-hearted. Other music makes us feel sad and serious.

How does a composer convey mood? He may use sprightly rhythms and lilting melodies to impart a feeling of gaiety. He may employ sustained tones and somber harmonies to create a feeling of melancholy. There are myriad devices and techniques at his command to project mood in musical terms.

Primary grades. For the primary child, physical response to music is one of the more direct ways for him to react to mood. After he has listened to the music a few times, ask him, "Can you show with your body how the music makes you feel?" He dramatizes songs and song stories to project a feeling of mood.

The primary child should learn to express mood through his singing. A happy song should sound happy, a sad song should sound sad. He learns that certain rhythm instruments match certain moods better than others. Why, for example, does a triangle sound better for "Twinkle, Twinkle, Little Star" than a drum?

With the help of his teacher, the child attempts to find words like "spooky, angry, quiet, or smooth" to describe a song or recording. He begins to develop a growing awareness of the parallel moods of the words and the melody.

Intermediate grades. In the intermediate grades the child should become increasingly aware of *how* the composer is able to project mood. What is the effect of major and minor? What does the selection of orchestral instruments have to do with mood? What effect does the text have on mood? What are the influences of harmony and rhythm on mood?

The child in the intermediate grades indicates mood by the manner in which he sings and plays. He interprets mood through performance. He comes to know some of the symbols used by the composer to assist the performer in achieving a desired mood.

Tone

In the elementary music program we learn that tone is the unique building material of music. Tone is distinguished from noise by the regularity of vibrations which results in definite pitch.

The elementary child comes to know tone because of these readily understood characteristics:

It has pitch. It is high or low.

It has duration. It lasts for a specific period of time, short or long.

It has intensity. It is loud or soft.

It has quality. It is different for each individual voice and individual instrument.

Primary grades. In the primary grades, the child learns to distinguish tone from noise. One good way to teach this is to call attention to the many sounds that he hears in his world and ask him to decide which are tones and which are noise. Can he name some high sounds? Some low sounds? What is the softest sound he can think of? The loudest? Some sounds are long while others are short. Can he suggest examples?

The primary child's early musical experiences include matching tones. He learns to sing with a pleasing tone and he becomes aware of expressive tones as he listens or as he makes music himself. Very early he begins to evaluate his singing as well as that of his classmates. He adapts physical movement to tone quality—heavy movement for big tones, delicate movement for light tones.

He learns what is meant by tone color through playing simple percussion and melody instruments. He is curious about how tone is produced and experiments with such tone-producers as tuned water glasses, stretched rubber bands, and a wide variety of improvised percussion instruments. He also develops a growing awareness of the relationship between tonal sound and musical notation.

Intermediate grades. The intermediate grade child is developing the ability to sing with a full, free-flowing, expressive tone. He sings with greater range and more accurate intonation. He is able to sing on pitch and with good resonance. He realizes that tone quality is directly related to style, that the tone quality for a hymn is quite different from that for a nonsense song.

He is beginning to identify the various tone colors or timbre of the standard orchestral instruments. From recordings he recognizes the distinctive characteristics of adult voices: soprano, alto, tenor, and bass. He is more discriminative in terms of tone quality in selecting melody, rhythm, and harmony instruments for use in classroom activities.

Melody

Melody is introduced to the elementary child as a rhythmically organized succession of single tones. Each tone has both pitch and duration. Elementary children should become aware very early of the "up-down" and "short-long" features of the melody line. Increasingly they will become aware of the fact that melodies progress by scale-wise movement, skip-wise movement, or repeated tones. Boys and girls should be able to follow the melodic contour both by sight and by sound.

Primary grades. The primary child learns to sing a melody in a smooth or detached manner as appropriate. He shows the rise and fall of the melody through hand and body movements and he is able to sense the loud-soft, high-low, short-long characteristics of the melodies he sings and plays. In addition to his singing experience, he learns more about melody through playing simple instruments such as melody bells, xylophones, tuned glasses, and resonator bells. Through keyboard experience he learns to use the piano as an audio-visual reference. He begins to observe that notes and tones go up, down, or stay the same. He observes that some notes are close together while others are far apart.

He learns about melody by completing an unfinished tune. He is also given the opportunity to make up short melodies to sing or play. He creates introductions and codas and improvises simple, repetitive ostinati to pentatonic melodies. He is able to identify steps, skips, and repeated tones. He is introduced to letter names, syllables, and scale degree numbers and he begins to develop a rudimentary awareness of tonal relationships.

Intermediate grades. The intermediate grade child is able to decide whether a melody should be sung *legato, staccato,* or *marcato* and is able to perform it accordingly. He is able to clap the basic pulse (beat) as well as the melodic rhythm. He is able to identify major, minor, and pentatonic melodies.

He gains an increased understanding of melodic construction through playing simple flute-like instruments including the recorder. He continues his keyboard experience. He creates song texts and melodies as a class undertaking as well as individually. He is given opportunities to make up descants, introductions, and codas. He comes to understand better the characteristics of melodic construction by making up his own songs.

Rhythm

An introduction to the study of rhythm would emphasize the concept that rhythm is the grouping or arranging of long and short tones, of heavy and light beats in music. Rhythm, in its broadest sense, is everything that has to do with the duration of musical sound.

Some of the basic elements of rhythm that are emphasized in the elementary music program include:

Beat   The pulse of music which measures intervals of time.

Accent   Stressed or emphasized beats.

Meter   The grouping of beats and accents in the rhythmic flow of music. This rhythmical pattern is indicated by the meter signature. For example, ¾ meter means that the basic rhythmical value is the quarter note and that there are three quarter notes in a measure.

Primary grades. The primary child learns about rhythm largely through physical movement. He walks, runs, skips, jumps, and sways in response to the basic swing of the music. He accompanies songs and chants with patting, tapping, and clapping. He indicates quarter, eighth, and half-note values through movement. He takes part in singing games and dances.

Rhythm instruments extend the physical responses. He uses rhythm instruments to accompany songs and recordings as well as for the accompaniment of physical movement. He makes up simple rhythmic patterns to accompany his songs. He also makes up rhythmic introductions and codas.

He learns to recognize quarter, eighth, and half-note patterns on the staff. He is able to read simple patterns made up of these note values.

Intermediate grades. The intermediate grade child comes to be increasingly aware that rhythm is an integral part of melody. He understands beat and accent and observes them in his singing. He is able to distinguish between even and uneven rhythms.

He continues to respond with fundamental movements to rhythm but he also participates more and more in organized folk dances. He builds a repertoire of representative dances of America as well as other countries.

In his listening he is able to distinguish between duple and triple meter. He hears repeated rhythmic patterns and he is able to recognize such representative dances as the waltz, minuet, gavotte, and polka.

He increases his skill in using rhythm instruments, particularly those of Latin America. He continues to respond creatively to rhythm and he is encouraged to make up simple dances.

In reading, he is able to sing and play dotted patterns and he acquires a feeling for and an ability to recognize syncopation in notation. He understands the common time signatures and is able to observe and follow tempo markings.

Form

To the elementary child, form in music means its design. When we refer to form we are speaking of the way in which music is put together. Children discover that there is a structure to a composition just as there is to a building.

Primary grades. The primary child realizes, through singing, that a song has a beginning, a middle, and an end. He becomes aware of the musical phrase as an important unit of form. He phrases music through movement and responds to cadences (pauses in the melodic flow) in a similar manner. Increasingly, he is aware that the movement patterns of simple dances correlate with musical form.

He begins to notice that some phrases sound alike and that others are different. He becomes aware that a composition takes on form through repetition (like phrases) and contrast (unlike phrases).

He uses instruments to point up repeated sections and contrasting phrases. He makes up "answer" phrases to "question" phrases. He is introduced to the concept of identifying sections by alphabetical letters so that he recognizes AB as a two-part form, ABA as three-part form.

Intermediate grades. The intermediate grade child is able to distinguish between phrases that are like, unlike, or similar. He is aware of sequences as well as cadences. In addition to indicating phrase length through movement, he begins to learn some simple conducting patterns for a better understanding of pulse and meter. He knows that the movement patterns of dance correlate with musical form.

In addition to being able to analyze simple AB and ABA construction, he is also familiar with the rondo as well as theme and variations. In his listening, he is introduced to excerpts from opera, ballet, and oratorio as well as examples from symphonic literature.

He uses instruments to emphasize design. He also uses melody instruments for accompanying, for antiphonal effects, and for one of the voices in a round. He makes up simple dances to illustrate musical form. He is able to identify form through listening and through notation. He is increasingly aware of the parallels between poetic and musical form.

Harmony

The child learns that harmony consists of tones sounded together. Although early experiences in harmony will be through listening, the older child will also experience harmony in playing as well as in part singing.

Primary grades. The primary child is introduced to harmony by hearing an accompaniment or listening to a recording. He may provide a very simple one or two note accompaniment on the bells while the class sings. Eventually, he plays independent second parts on melody instruments.

He prepares for part singing by singing simple descants, repeated melodic motives as second parts, and rounds. Through singing and listening he becomes aware of *do* or l as the stopping place for a song. He is able to distinguish between the sound of the I chord and the V chord when played on the piano or autoharp.

Intermediate grades. The intermediate grade child experiences harmony directly through part-singing. At first he sings simple descants, repeated melodic motives, parallel harmonies, chord roots and, eventually, part-song arrangements.

He is able to differentiate by sound between the I, IV, and V chords and he is able to make up harmonic accompaniments using these chords on the autoharp. In so doing, he comes to realize the close relationship that exists between the melody and its implied, supporting harmony. With his ability to play bells, flutes, and other simple melody instruments, he is able to use them for descants, chord roots, and second parts.

He is able to locate the keynote from the signature. He knows the whole-step and half-step patterns for major and minor, and he begins to become aware of transposition and modulation.

Implications for the Specialist

In substance, then, we are pointing out that a concern for the traditionally accepted activities or approaches to musical learning is not, in and of itself, enough. True, it is important that we have a variety of approaches to music understanding. "What do we *do* in elementary music?" is a significant question. We want children to sing many types of songs. We want them to respond physically to music. We want them to listen to music of many styles, of many periods, of many countries. We want them to play a variety of melody, rhythm, and harmony instruments. We want them to make up melodies, words, and rhythms. We hope that they will become increasingly literate in their ability to read the musical score.

However, we must also face up to the question, "If the children *do* all of these things, *what* will they *learn?*" It is perfectly clear that the elementary music specialist cannot hope to teach the elements of mood, tone, melody, rhythm, form, and harmony in a short period of time any more than she can teach children how to sing, move, listen, play, create, and read in a few lessons. What we are recommending is that she needs guidelines and some kind of check-list for musical learnings just as much as she needs them for musical activities.

For example, Miss Carol Jones periodically evaluates her teaching in terms of the *musical learnings* that her children are achieving. In fact, her evaluation is even more concerned with learnings than it is with activities. Although the guidelines for musical learnings apply to all approaches, let us consider how Miss Jones would use them in her singing program.

She would be sure that her children are able to project the *mood* of the song in the way in which they sing. She makes certain that the children's repertoire of songs represents many moods. She sees to it that major, minor, pentatonic, and modal melodies are included in the singing program and that the relationship of mode to mood is explored. Her children sing songs of many historical periods and of many geographical areas. In the upper grades, boys and girls investigate some of the devices a composer uses in a song to project mood.

In her concern for *tone,* Miss Jones makes certain that her boys and girls sing with an unforced, natural, pleasing quality. In the primary grades she helps boys and girls find their singing voices through tone-matching and tone-play. At all levels, she encourages them to sit or stand with good posture to facilitate good tone production. As the child progresses in the grades, she is increasingly concerned with his ability to sing with good resonance and accurate intonation. Her children extend their control of dynamics in singing. They also increase the range of their voices.

There are many aspects of *melody* that may be taught through classroom singing. The relationship of the text to the melody is a highly significant learning. In the primary grades the children decide whether a given melody should be sung smoothly or in a detached manner. In the upper elementary grades this learning is refined to an understanding of *legato, marcato,* and *staccato.* The concept of melodic contour and melodic climax may be taught effectively through singing. Miss Jones illustrates tonal tendencies in her classroom activities. Older children experience the sound of simultaneous melodies in rounds, descants, and part-songs.

Basic concepts of *rhythm* are taught through song. Miss Jones teaches her primary children to sing in a steady rhythm and to sing fast, slow, or moderately as appropriate. Through singing, children are able to tell whether the music "swings" in twos or threes. Her older children distinguish between duple and triple meter. They also know that songs are sung fast or slow for expressive reasons. Children realize that rhythm is as vital to melody as pitch. In the upper grades they are introduced to syncopation and note the effect of displaced accents in their songs.

The primary child first becomes aware of *form* through song. He comes to know what phrases are and he begins to understand that a song takes on form through phrase repetition and contrast. He learns to sing a phrase on one breath. In the upper grades he begins to note obvious sequences and he recognizes the cadences or pauses in the melodic flow. He becomes more and more skillful in analyzing the forms of the songs he sings.

Miss Jones knows that the primary grade child's first contact with *harmony* in singing will be through hearing accompaniments. He learns to sing with a variety of accompaniments including the piano, the autoharp, and recordings. He sings a single note against a melody and begins to sing some simple descants and harmony parts. In the intermediate grades he experiences harmony in song by singing rounds, by improvising harmony parts, by vocal chording, by adding descants, and by singing part-songs.

Of course, Miss Jones will keep in mind the six major musical learnings that we have identified as the children move to music, as they listen, as they play classroom instruments, as they create, and as they read music. It is not enough that she plans for a variety of activities. She must also bear in mind the musical learnings that she hopes boys and girls will achieve.

In our next chapter, we shall combine the concerns for both musical approaches and musical learnings by presenting them in a sequential, grade-by-grade organization.

Summary

Music educators are in general agreement that a wide variety of activities or approaches to musical learnings should be included in an elementary music program. The activities that are generally accepted are: singing, moving, listening, playing, creating, and reading. These activities should not be thought of as though they are tightly compartmentalized. They are complementary rather than mutually exclusive.

Musical learnings are the end results, the goals, and the objectives of musical activities. We must be as concerned with *what* is taught in the elementary program as we are with *how* it is taught. A set of guide-lines for musical learnings has not been commonly established nor widely accepted by music educators. We are suggesting six that we feel should be emphasized in elementary music: *mood, tone, melody, rhythm, form,* and *harmony.*

It is true, as with the approaches, that the learnings cannot be compartmentalized. It is readily conceded that this is not a definitive list of learnings although it is an appropriate one. In the elementary program we can hope to do little more than introduce the child to each of these learnings. It is very important that the desired learnings be constantly related to the developmental abilities of boys and girls in the classroom.

The main point of this chapter is that the elementary music specialist must be as concerned with what the children *learn* as what they *do*. It is not enough to see that the program provides for singing, for moving in response to music, for listening, for playing classroom instruments, for creating, and for reading. We must also make sure that children are responding to mood and learning about tone, about melody, about rhythm, about form, and about harmony.

Questions for Discussion

1. The usual activities in the elementary music program are singing, moving, listening, playing, creating, and reading. The point is made in this chapter that a concern for the activities is not enough. Explain.

2. What are the six categories of musical learnings established in this chapter? Can you suggest other categories?

3. At the sixth grade level, suggest some of the devices a composer uses to establish a mood that the boys and girls can appreciate and understand.

4. What may we teach the primary child about tone?

5. One criticism of the singing of children in the elementary classroom is that the songs sound very much alike no matter what they are about. Describe how you would convey an understanding of *marcato, legato,* and *staccato* to fourth grade children.

6. We usually define a meter signature as follows: "$\frac{6}{8}$ means that there are six eighth notes in a measure and every eighth note gets one beat." What is incorrect about this definition? How might we define it?

7. Do you subscribe to the practice of referring to quarter notes as "walking" notes and eighth notes as "running" notes? Cite some advantages and disadvantages.

8. Percussive instruments are widely used in the primary grades. Suggest what we might do to provide for their greater utilization in the upper elementary grades.

9. Besides using the autoharp and singing part songs, outline some procedures for experiencing harmony in the fifth and sixth grades.

10. Indicate how a checklist that includes the six categories of musical learnings and the traditionally accepted music activities would be helpful in evaluating an elementary music program.

8

Organizing
Musical Learnings

We need to emphasize the musical *learnings* we hope to achieve to the same degree that we have concerned ourselves with *approaches* to musical understanding. We also need to "spell out" both approaches and learnings in some kind of developmental sequence.

This is a challenging and, at the same time, a presumptuous undertaking. It is challenging because there is not a common agreement for attainments in elementary music education to the extent that there is in language arts, social studies, or mathematics. And in the areas of physical education and arts and crafts the expected outcomes of the elementary program are more clearly delineated than they are in music education.

To attempt to organize a sequential pattern is presumptuous because, in the first place, there is a wide range of expectancies on the part of general educators as far as the elementary music program is concerned. In the second place, music educators themselves are far from being in unanimous agreement as to what musical learnings should be emphasized in the elementary school. However, we shall be both forward and presumptuous by setting forth what we consider to be reasonable objectives in a developmental sequence.

This task is based on several assumptions. These basic assumptions are:

1. It is understood that the following learnings are not exhaustive or exclusive. Additional items could well be added. The learnings have been selected on the

basis of their immediacy, appropriateness, and musical significance. Despite the selectivity, it is recognized that the list is extensive. An excellent music program may not include all of the learnings listed.

2. Placement by grade levels is on an empirical basis. A sequence of learnings might be rearranged. A learning suggested for the fourth grade might be taught in some situations as early as the second grade. In other schools, the same learning might be appropriate for the fifth grade.

3. The practice of assigning learnings by grade levels is, in itself, suspect. Several interesting experiments have been made where music is taught on the basis of developmental readiness without regard for grade-level lines. In these experimental programs children are grouped according to their ability to learn and to perform, not on the basis of chronological age. However, almost every music specialist works within the framework of grade levels. For this reason, the traditional grade groupings are recognized.

4. It is understood that the learnings as listed are not compartmentalized. Actually, many learnings may be going on at the same time. When the second grade child dramatizes the mood of a song, he is singing, moving, and listening to music. In addition to mood, he may be aware of rhythm, melody, and form. Learnings are not mutually exclusive. They augment and reinforce each other.

5. The learnings must be considered not only sequentially but cyclically. They are arranged with a regard for developmental readiness, but each learning must be reinforced many times. For example, a second-grade learning, "Understand and observe these symbols: *p, mf, f,*" must be repeated and reinforced in the second grade and in later grades if it is to be firmly established.

6. Perhaps most important of all, it must be understood that musical responsiveness is not an accumulation of isolated bits of music making. It involves the total musical act experienced by the individual.

On the following pages, the musical goals are developed grade level by grade level. Each grade is divided into the six recognized approaches: singing, moving, listening, playing, creating, and reading. Within these categories, the musical learnings—mood, tone, rhythm, melody, harmony, and form—have been given due emphasis.

Participation Important for All Grade Levels

Many learnings are of such a nature that they need to be emphasized at *every level*. For example, the goal to "sing expressively" is not unique for any one grade. It is as appropriate in the first grade as it is for the professional artist in his mature years. These are the common musical learnings that should be emphasized at all levels in the elementary school:

Singing:

Sing expressively.

Sing phrasewise, with good diction, in correct rhythm.

Sit or stand with good posture.

Sing smoothly (*legato*) or detached (*staccato*) as appropriate.

Sing alone as well as in a group.

Sing major, minor, pentatonic, and modal songs.

Sing with a variety of accompaniments.

Moving:

Respond to music creatively through large, free movements.

Dramatize music through movement.

Indicate phrasing and form through movement.

Develop, through movement, a feeling for accented and unaccented beats.

Participate in singing games and dances.

Listening:

Learn to listen attentively to music.

Identify mood through listening.

Listen while singing, playing, and moving to music.

Become familiar with the timbre of voices and orchestral instruments.

Become aware of strong and weak beats in music and poetry.

Listen to major, minor, pentatonic, and modal melodies.

Playing:

Play rhythm and melody instruments.

Select instruments to match mood.

Use instruments to accompany songs.

Use instruments to accompany movement.

Use instruments for sound effects in songs, stories, poems, or dramatizations.

Improvise *ostinati* (short, repeated melodic patterns).

Take part in keyboard experience.

Creating:

Create free and patterned movement.

Make up answer phrases to question phrases.

Complete simple chants, texts, and songs.

Make up rhythmic patterns to accompany songs.

Make up songs and instrumental melodies.

Select appropriate instruments to accompany singing and dancing.

Reading:

Become aware of the relationship of the sound of music to the appearance of the printed page.

Become increasingly familiar with the musical staff, musical terms, and symbols.

Take part in choral speaking.

Musical Goals for Grade One

Many six-year-old children are stepping for the first time beyond the friendly, familiar boundaries of family life into the school and community.

The first-grade child is faced with a significant developmental task in making new friends and finding his place in a new group. Perhaps for the first time, he will be a part of a social group made up of peers rather than adults.

Music can help very much in making this transition from home to school. When encouraging him to respond to music physically, it is important to bear in mind that his small muscles are not as well developed as his larger muscles. It is difficult for the six-year-old to do precise movements without considerable effort.

However, physical activity is the predominant characteristic. He involves his body in everything he does. It is difficult for him to be still for any length of time. Music activities in the first grade should be directly related to physical movement.

His creative efforts will be crude by adult standards but they should be accepted, respected, and encouraged. Six-year-olds are competitive and there will be considerable striving for first place.

The six-year-old child enjoys spontaneous play. Informal "acting out" is so typical a part of his self-play that it would be foolish indeed not to capitalize on this interest in the classroom.

He is eager to learn and likes to assume responsibility. Decisions are hard to make and he should not be asked to make too many either-or choices. He needs love, affection, warmth, and friendliness. His biggest task is to feel "at home" in his new school situation.

As at any level, there is a great range in physical, emotional, and intellectual maturation. Some six-year-olds are still "babies." Others are quite self-reliant little people.

These are the musical goals appropriate for the first grade:

Singing:

Sing many short, simple songs.
Learn to sing with a pleasing, unforced tone quality.
Match tones.
Learn to express mood through the way one sings.

Moving:

Respond to music physically with large, free movements.
Take part in action songs and singing games.
Dramatize or pantomime reaction to mood.
Show the rise and fall of melody through hand and body movement.
Show phrases in music through movement.

Listening:

Become aware of the many sounds in his world, distinguish between tone and noise.
Listen for differences in high and low, loud and soft, short and long in songs and recordings.

Listen as he sings, plays, and moves to music.

Learn to listen to some music quietly and attentively.

Playing:

Learn to keep time to music with rhythm instruments.

Be introduced to melody instruments such as song bells, resonator bells, psaltery, and xylophone.

Play simple patterns by ear, blank notation, and number.

Make and play some simple instruments.

Creating:

Pantomime, dramatize a song or recording.

Make up answer phrases to question phrases.

Decide which rhythm or melody instruments should be used to accompany a song.

Decide what the mood of a song or recording is.

Reading:

Read the text of a simple song.

Become aware of the directions at the beginning of a song: slowly, smoothly, fast, etc.

Notice that one's voice goes up, down, or stays on the same pitch, as notes on the staff go up, down, or stay the same.

Musical Goals for Grade Two

The seven-year-old child has great energy and vitality. The vigorous physical movement of his play calls for compensating periods of rest. In music activities for the second grade there is a need for quiet listening as well as opportunities for physical response.

He is able to read words with some independence. The first music-reading experiences centering on high-low, short-long belong at this level. He is interested in fairy tales and myths of all kinds. These interests should be reflected in the texts of many of the songs he sings.

Like the six-year-old, he is aggressive but he is more sensitive to the feelings of others. He seeks a friend of the same sex but he is still very much in need of teacher approval and encouragement from other adults who are close to him. He is anxious to do well and he tends to be quite critical of himself. The seven-year-old is responsive and eager to take on new ideas. He is working toward increasing independence and self-reliance.

In addition to extending the learning experiences for the first grade, the musical learnings appropriate for the second grade are:

Singing:

Sing songs smoothly or detached as appropriate.

Sing a phrase on one breath.

Sing so the meaning of the text is understood.
Sing in steady rhythm.

Moving:

Dramatize songs and song-stories.
Take part in singing games and simple dances.
Carry out movements suggested in texts of songs.
Respond to the basic swing of the music through physical movement.
Indicate quarter, eighth, and half note values through movement.

Listening:

Become aware of and feel strong and weak beats.
Become aware of the grouping of pulses in twos and threes.
Determine the predominant mood of a song or recording.
Recognize repetition of the melody.
Listen to many kinds of music expressing many moods.

Playing:

Select rhythm and melody instruments to match mood.
Begin to play simple autoharp accompaniments.
Play repetitive rhythmic patterns and melodic patterns (*ostinati*) while the class sings.
Experiment with objects that produce tone: water glasses, bottles, bells, etc.
Use instruments to emphasize important words of the text.

Creating:

Complete an unfinished melody.
Suggest additional words for a song text.
Make up descriptive titles for recordings.
Answer a rhythmic question by clapping or playing.
Make up simple rhythmic patterns to accompany songs.

Reading:

Become acquainted with quarter, eighth, and half notes.
Become acquainted with the treble staff.
Become acquainted with numbers and the *so-fa* syllables.
Recognize stepwise, skipwise, and repeated note patterns.
Observe like and unlike patterns and phrases.
Read simple stepwise patterns, patterns based on the I chord (1-3-5 or *do-mi-so*).

Musical Goals for Grade Three

In many ways, the third grade is a dividing line between early childhood and a child's more mature middle years. The eight-year-old does not want to be "babied" but he still needs a great deal of adult support and encouragement.

His arms are lengthening, his hands are larger, and his eye-hand co-ordination is improved. He is able to manipulate simple rhythm, melody, and harmony instruments with considerably more dexterity than in the earlier two grades.

The boys are still very active physically. "Rough and tumble" play is the norm. Girls are not quite as inclined to strike out physically as they did in the earlier grades. There is a growing sense of peer loyalty and some gangs and clubs may begin to form.

Most children now read prose independently. This is a good grade level to focus attention on music reading skills. Third grade children are quite receptive to such concepts as the *so-fa* syllables.

The eight-year-old child has an improved concept of time. He is developing an interest in the "long ago." He looks beyond the immediate child world to wider horizons. He is interested in children of other lands.

He sees himself more clearly in relation to others. He realizes that some children do things better than he but he also knows that there are some activities in which he excels. He is extremely curious and eager to learn more of the world about him.

In addition to extending the learning experiences of the first two grades, the musical learnings appropriate for the third grade are:

Singing:

Extend singing range, increase resonance.
Decide, on his own, whether a song should be sung smoothly or in a detached syle.
Sing simple descants, rounds, and canons in two parts.
Begin to acquire a varied song repertoire of lasting value.

Moving:

Do a variety of folk dances.
Indicate phrase length through movement.
Develop through movement a feeling for accented and unaccented beats.
Clap rhythmic patterns from notation.

Listening:

Be introduced to the sound of the basic instruments in each orchestral family: violin, trumpet, clarinet and drum.
Listen to choral as well as instrumental recordings.
Identify simple two- and three-part construction: AB, ABA.
Recognize duple and triple meter by sound.
Distinguish between the sound of the I, IV, and V chords played on the piano or autoharp.

Playing:

Play simple melodies from notation on bells, xylophone, piano.
Play simple descants and second parts.
Play one rhythmic pattern while others sing or play a different pattern.
Select proper chord (I, IV, or V) to accompany songs on the autoharp.

Creating:

Make up rhythm patterns to accompany songs.
Complete unfinished melodies and texts.
Make up melodies for short poems.
Make up a text for a short melody.
Add simple introductions and codas to songs.
Make up simple dance patterns.

Reading:

Observe the tempo indication at the beginning of a song.
Note that a musical phrase is usually one line of a poem.
Be familiar with lines, spaces, letter names of treble staff.
Be introduced to whole-steps, half-steps and the major scale pattern.
Understand ²⁄₄, ³⁄₄, and ⁴⁄₄ meter.
Understand slurs and ties.

Musical Goals for Grade Four

The nine-year-old child is a youngster who can be dependable and responsible. Strong interests are beginning to develop. Individual differences in musical abilities are as obvious as differences in other abilities.

His eye-hand coordination is good and the small muscles of his hands are well developed and well coordinated. The simple flute-like instruments are most effective when introduced at this level.

His attention span has increased to the point where the teacher may spend a considerably longer time on a particularly absorbing topic. He is still active in his play. The differences in play interests of boys and girls are more clearly marked than in the primary grades.

He is quite critical of himself, in fact, he may be something of a perfectionist. The texts of his songs should reflect his waning interest in fantasy and fairy tales and his increased interest in relating himself to the here-and-now: his community, his state, his nation. He is beginning to evidence strong feelings of pride in his country. This is a good level to emphasize the singing of patriotic songs.

He responds best when treated as an individual in an adult way. He likes to be included in planning. He is increasingly able to make intelligent decisions on the basis of his own experience. However, the teacher must not overestimate his maturity since he vacillates between the young and middle-age child roles.

The interest in clubs and gangs is stronger. Peer loyalty is greater and he depends less on adults. This is a year of relatively good adjustment. The child is fairly steady, almost as though he is readying himself for the more turbulent pre-adolescent and adolescent years that are to follow.

In addition to extending the learning experiences of the first three grades, the musical learnings appropriate for the fourth grade are:

Singing:

Sing dialogue songs.

Sing *legato, staccato,* or *marcato* as appropriate.

Sing some two-part songs including rounds, canons, descants, chord roots, and parallel harmonies.

Sing some three-part rounds.

Be aware of melodic contour and melodic climax.

Moving:

Do American square dances.

Clap the melodic rhythm from notation.

Be aware that dance patterns correlate with musical form.

Act out simple rounds.

Listening:

Identify like and unlike phrases by sound as well as by sight.

Recognize simple rondo form; e.g., ABACA.

Extend recognition of sounds of orchestral instruments.

Observe how instruments contribute to mood.

Distinguish between major and minor by sound.

Playing:

Play simple melody-wind instruments including the recorder.

Extend the use of melody, rhythm, and harmony instruments.

Accompany songs and dances.

Use melody instruments as one voice in a round.

Use instruments to indicate form.

Creating:

Make up accompaniments for the autoharp.

Make up melodies for short poems.

Make up a simple song, words and music.

Improvise harmony parts by ear.

Combine several songs into a playlet.

Reading:

Understand dynamic symbols from *pp* to *ff*.

Learn to locate the keynote.

Understand the time signatures in his book.

Understand chromatic symbols: sharp, flat, and natural.

Use melody instruments in the reading program.

Be introduced to the minor scale, continue study of major.

Musical Goals for Grade Five

This is a somewhat difficult, unpredictable year. There is a wide, obvious divergence in physical maturation. Some ten-year-olds may be well into the pre-puberty growth spurt. This is especially true of girls who are, on the average, one or two years more mature than boys in physiological growth.

This more mature development of girls is also reflected in attitudes and interests in the classroom. It shows up dramatically in music activities. The girls' positive attitude toward folk dancing, for example, is not shared by most of the boys. The teacher must provide for early maturers as well as for late maturers in classroom activities.

Physical "laziness" may be in part the result of fatigue due to the rapid growth spurt. There are, of course, concomitant emotional changes. There is some criticism of the teacher and a resistance to adult authority. "Crushes" and "hero worship" are common. The gang-group feeling is reflected by a high degree of interest in team sports.

In addition to extending the learning experiences of the first four grades, the musical learnings appropriate for the fifth grade are:

Singing:

Combine melodies: second parts, descants, canons, partner-songs.

Sing three-part and some four-part rounds.

Learn to blend and balance in part singing.

Sing *rubato* when appropriate.

Begin to build a permanent song repertoire.

Moving:

Dramatize ballad-type songs.

Perform couple dances.

Extend square-dance and folk-dance repertoire.

Begin to learn basic conducting patterns: in two, in three, in four.

Listening:

Begin to listen to two parts simultaneously.

Recognize the melody line in a recording of the full orchestra.

Identify meter through listening.

Begin to build a permanent listening repertoire.

Playing:

Play melody instruments in two parts.

Use melody instruments to play one of the voices in a part-song.

Participate in a classroom orchestra including melody, rhythm, and harmony instruments.

Play chordal accompaniments on the piano and autoharp.

Creating:

Interpret a song effectively.

Improvise by ear.

Make up an instrumental melody.

Create a round of rhythmic patterns.

Choose from his listening repertoire a selection that fits the mood of a story, a poem, or a picture.

Reading:

Extend reading ability to include skips between intervals not in the tonic chord, particularly the fourth and the sixth.

Measure intervals.

Study major and minor scale construction.

Be introduced to syncopated rhythms.

Understand the lyrics as a pre-requisite to interpreting a song.

Musical Goals for Grade Six

Differences in physiological development are even more apparent among eleven-year-old children. Nearly all of the girls are taller and heavier than boys and secondary sex characteristics are more pronounced. Some girls' voices may begin to change. Many boys want to sing "lower" even though their voices are unchanged. Few boys are willing to be identified as sopranos.

Girls' interest in the boys increases and some boys will begin to be concerned about what the girls think of them. There is a great need to conform to the expectations of the peer group. Peer approval is now a stronger motivating force than adult approval, including the approval of the teacher.

Each child is working very hard at the task of being accepted by others. Group activities in music, particularly square and folk dancing, are appealing to most children at this level.

Eleven-year-olds participate enthusiastically in organized team sports. This is especially true of boys but also, to a lesser degree, of girls. They enjoy directed experiences in musical games and dances. Elementary choirs, bands, and orchestras provide outlets for this interest. They realize that, regardless of personal wishes, they must accept the responsibility to the group. Music activities offer many opportunities to learn to subordinate individual desires for group goals. This is a self-discipline of great value to the eleven-year-old child.

There are some indications of an emerging vocational interest. "What are you going to be when you grow up?" is asked frequently. This is one example of the child reaching up to the adult world as he begins to orient himself socially. Many children of this age are listening to adult-level music. They appreciate and respond to music far beyond their ability to perform. The eleven-year-old is on the threshold of adolescence and some early maturers have already entered this phase of their development.

The sixth grader likes to do things well. An effective music program encourages the child to perform to the best of his ability. There is no "ceiling" on musical achievement.

In addition to extending the learning experiences of the first five grades, the musical learnings appropriate for the sixth grade are:

Singing:

Sing many unison songs, some two- and three-part songs.
Sing four-part rounds.
Sing songs with crossing parts.
"Chord" in three parts.

Moving:

Do many dances of his own and other countries.
Clap one rhythmic pattern while classmates are clapping other rhythmic patterns.
Conduct some songs using standard conducting patterns.
Act out a four-part round.

Listening:

Note some of the more obvious devices a composer uses to achieve mood.
Listen to examples of opera, ballet, oratorio, and symphonic literature.
Be able to hear another part while singing or playing his own part.
Recognize the sound of adult voices: soprano, alto, tenor, bass.
Recognize the orchestral choirs: strings, wood-winds, brass, percussion.

Playing:

Play some of the songs in his book.
Use melody instruments for chording, for second parts.
Play characteristic percussion instruments of other countries.
Use standard band and orchestra instruments to enrich classroom music activities.

Creating:

Decide how a song should be interpreted.
Make up and notate original rhythmic patterns.

Make up and notate a song or instrumental melody.

Make up patterned dances.

Create a rhythmic round.

Reading:

Use numbers and/or syllables with some facility.

Be able to read step-wise patterns, patterns built on the I and V chords, intervals of the fourth and sixth.

Identify even and uneven rhythms.

Consider unusual meter signatures (e.g., ⅝) that appear in his book.

Summary

The musical *learnings* that we hope to achieve in the elementary school must be as well established as the *approaches* to musical understanding. In this chapter, we have "spelled out" these learnings, keeping in mind (1) that the list is not definitive, (2) that variations are possible in assignment to grade levels, (3) that experiments have been made in grouping children on the basis of understanding and ability rather than chronological age, (4) that the learnings cannot be compartmentalized, and (5) that learnings must be reinforced in a cyclical manner.

Musical goals were presented for each grade level since the great majority of elementary music specialists work within this framework. Each grade was divided into the six established activities or approaches: singing, moving, listening, playing, creating, and reading. Within this organization, aspects of mood, tone, rhythm, melody, harmony, and form were considered as musical goals at each level.

Participation for *all* grade levels was considered. A brief description of significant characteristics of the child's development at the chronological ages of six, seven, eight, nine, ten, and eleven was given. These developmental characteristics were related to the elementary music program and to specific musical goals for grades one, two, three, four, five, and six.

Questions for Discussion

1. What do you think of grouping children on the basis of musical ability rather than by grade levels? What are some of the problems involved? What are the advantages?

2. Discuss this statement: "Musical responsiveness is not an accumulation of isolated bits of music making."

3. Is the musculature of the six-year-old child uniformly developed? What are the implications for the first grade music program?

4. Suggest experiences in music reading for the second grade.

5. Research studies indicate that children are most receptive to the *so-fa* syllables at the third grade level. Why do you suppose this is so?

6. Several of the current series recommend the introduction of simple winds (song flutes, tonettes, etc.) at the fourth-grade level. Other series recommend their introduction in third grade. What is your opinion? What is the basis for your answer?

7. Girls usually mature earlier than boys. What problems does this pose for the elementary music specialist in fifth and sixth grades?

8. What is meant by building a "permanent song repertoire" in elementary music?

9. How is the recorder being used in elementary music education today? Why do you suppose the recorder is enjoying such a vogue with musical amateurs?

10. Why is it wise to avoid the use of "soprano" and "alto" in part singing in the upper grades?

9

How Does the Consultant
Plan and Organize?

Thus far we have outlined the role of the consultant and the scope of her responsibilities, but we have not considered how she plans and organizes her daily work. The consultant may have a clear idea of what she hopes to accomplish in general terms but there still remains the problem of translating generalizations into day-by-day teaching.

Both long-range and short-range planning are essential for any creative endeavor. Up to this point we have taken long-range planning into account by indicating the need for continuing aims, by relating music to the overall objectives of elementary education, by considering the unique contributions that music education makes to personality fulfillment, and by examining approaches to musical understanding as well as musical learnings themselves. Such a long-range look at the job is necessary. Let us now turn our attention to translating long-range objectives into a plan of action that may be used by the elementary music consultant in her everyday work.

Planning the Work

Any undertaking should be approached as an entity before one attempts to break it down into smaller segments. In reading a textbook, for example, we get an idea of what the book is about from the title and the introductory material. If the chapters are grouped into several major sections we should know what they are. The author's chapter-by-chapter organization should be understood before we begin reading the text itself. Within each chapter, the major topics set forth the author's main ideas in outline form. With this kind of overview, we may begin reading sentence-by-sentence with real understanding. We are better able to comprehend the details from having first apprehended the whole.

In a similar fashion, the consultant, once she realizes how her job relates to the total educational endeavor, may proceed more intelligently to break down the task into workable segments. Although there are many different ways for the elementary music consultant to plan her work, we shall first consider the obvious but practical procedure of her planning work in conformity with the school year. We shall then proceed to sketch how she might go about preparing more detailed short-range plans.

We approach this task on the safe assumption that the elementary music consultant will be the person most concerned about planning her own work. However, it is certainly excellent practice to involve others concerned. Teachers and principals, in particular, should have an opportunity not only to react to the consultant's plans, but to work with her in formulating them.

Annual planning. The consultant must decide, from the great many choices that are available to her, the specific objectives for this *school year*. From the many possibilities as to what *might* be done, the consultant needs to identify those specific goals that *are* to be accomplished this year.

For example, Miss Carol Jones, in looking at her past work and evaluating her present situation, feels that these are her basic objectives for the current school year:

1. To familiarize elementary teachers with the new music textbooks that were adopted last May.
2. To outline a series of individual monthly plans that will focus on each of these musical learnings in turn: mood, tone, melody, rhythm, harmony, and form.
3. To provide more reading experiences in the classroom, particularly in grades four through six.
4. To continue to work with other music consultants, elementary teachers, and the supervisor of music in completing a curriculum guide for the Central City Schools.
5. To organize an in-service music group at Broadmoor Elementary School.
6. To implement the grade level objectives in music developed by the Lakeview Elementary School faculty in their in-service study group last year.

These objectives are specific. They do not cover the entire gamut of things that could be done. However, in Miss Jones' opinion, they are those things of greatest import in her situation that should be accomplished *this year*. They may not be appropriate objectives for Miss Jones next year or two years from now. But they are valid objectives as she begins *this* school year.

Far too many consultants begin the year's work without giving much thought to concrete goals. The consultant must begin with a number of specific goals in mind or she will proceed aimlessly. It is extremely important that the consultant think through objectives to the point that they are so clearly identified that she is able to write them down.

Although goals must be specific, they must also be flexible. For example, to Miss Jones' pleasant surprise, Mr. Robert Hawkins, the principal of Broadmoor Elementary School, placed an order during the summer for a complete record library designed for the elementary listening program. Miss Jones had recommended the library to Mr. Hawkins but there seemed little likelihood of obtaining it with the instructional funds then available. Although Miss Jones had not provided for the use of these records in her year's planning, it would be foolish indeed not to include them. To acquaint the teachers at Broadmoor Elementary School with the new record library and to spend the necessary time in showing them how to use it is an important new objective for Miss Jones at this school this year.

Monthly planning. To successfully achieve annual objectives, the consultant's planning must be broken down into smaller segments. Not only do the annual objectives relate to constant, continuing aims but they also serve as the framework for more detailed planning. In Miss Jones' case, she finds it helpful to divide her year's work into monthly and weekly planning.

The year's outline of work should serve as a skeletal outline to give point, purpose, and direction to the day-by-day work. This does not mean that responses, emerging interests, or requests that arise during the course of the year will be ignored in deference to the preconceived plan. Any intelligent plan allows for and encourages flexibility. But the consultant who begins her work in September with no idea in mind as to what she hopes to accomplish by May will soon find herself so engulfed by the daily routine that she will be unable to see beyond the next visit. Teaching without planning is almost certain to be chaotic and disorganized.

During the past several years Miss Jones has mapped out her monthly planning in different ways. One year she organized her work on the approaches to musical understanding. For example, for one month she focused her energies on playing classroom instruments. This did not mean that she eliminated all other music-making activities, but she did emphasize the playing of simple instruments at all levels in a wide variety of ways.

In carrying out this particular approach, Miss Jones discovered additional ways that instruments could be used in the upper elementary grades. She learned that there are many ways in which rhythm, melody, and harmony instruments are uniquely suited to grades four, five, and six. Primary rhythm instruments, for example, become percussive instruments used in a "grown-up" manner in the sixth grade classroom. The findings may not have been revolutionary, but they were new to Miss Jones and to her teachers.

Following her concentrated attention to playing instruments, Miss

Jones shifted her emphasis the following month to the listening program. Again, without excluding other approaches, she highlighted listening activities. She not only brought to the classroom fresh ideas for teachers and rich experiences for children, but through the deliberate emphasis given to this phase of the program, she also discovered new insights and developed new concepts.

Miss Jones' objectives for the "listening" month were:

1. Check with the elementary principals concerning recordings available in each building.
2. Use a recorded selection as a part of each classroom visit this month if it is at all possible to do so.
3. Encourage teachers to play recordings between visits.
4. Explore ways in which recordings may be used to exemplify mood, tone, melody, rhythm, harmony, and form.
5. Use the listening examples included in the basic music series.

Miss Jones emphasized other approaches in other months. In each instance, singing or creating or reading or moving to music became the focal but not the exclusive interest. For example, when the playing of instruments was emphasized, the children also sang, moved to music, read, listened, and created.

Next year, Miss Jones plans to use quite a different approach. The musical learnings themselves—mood, tone, melody, rhythm, harmony, and form—will become the organizing framework. For example, during one month Miss Jones will explore with her teachers and with the boys and girls the many ways that music is able to express mood. What is meant by mood in music? What are the unique capabilities that music has to convey mood? What are some of its limitations? These and many other questions will be considered, discussed, and exemplified.

The following month, Miss Jones will highlight musical experiences that point up form. Primary children will come to know phrases through body movement. Sixth graders will be introduced to the formal structure of the simple rondo. In other months, rhythm, melody, tone, and harmony may serve as central topics.

In establishing a focal point each month, Miss Jones is careful to see that other considerations are not avoided or ignored. Emerging interests of children, unexpected competencies developed by teachers, and provisions for additional materials of instruction are factors that may alter a carefully made plan. But there must be a plan of organization which all understand. Miss Jones, like any professional, is involved in a life-long process of probing, analyzing, refining, and improving. Planning is absolutely essential for the success of the elementary music program in the schools she serves.

Any monthly plan, no matter what the scheme of organization may be, will provide for the recurring patterns of the school calendar. Holidays, seasonal activities, and traditional school performances are taken into account.

There is, of course, no one best way to organize monthly planning. Too many variables are involved to suggest a reliable formula. The adoption of a new series, for example, requires special attention. Implementing basic concepts suggested in professional literature is a major accomplishment. A study of the relationship of music with art, physical education, or other subject areas demands thoughtful planning. Often the broader objectives of a system-wide study may have implications for music education. A topic adopted by the instructional staff such as "Relating the Expressed Interests of Children to Curriculum Development" would be as relevant for music education as for any other area of the curriculum.

Regardless of the plan selected, it will almost certainly be revised, refined, extended, and altered as the year progresses. However, it is of crucial importance that Miss Jones establishes central objectives and that she defines them to the point that she is able to summarize them in writing. They are as essential to her day-by-day work as a skeletal outline is for a major piece of writing.

Weekly planning. How far should the consultant go in her weekly planning? To what extent should each visit to the classroom be planned?

The consultant needs to avoid two extremes: (1) going into the classroom with no plan whatsoever and only a hazy notion of what she will do after her cheery "Good morning, boys and girls," and (2) having a detailed plan that is so finely timed and so carefully rehearsed that there is no possibility of adjusting to a spontaneous reaction of children or to interests of the teacher.

In our discussion of weekly planning, we are considering plans made for successive visits to any one room. The majority of elementary music consultants are able to visit each of their classrooms on a weekly basis. If more frequent or less frequent visits are made the planning will, of course, need to be adjusted accordingly.

Perhaps we might clarify our thinking by examining a page from Miss Jones' notebook:

October, Second Week.

Emphasis: listening.

A. Sing a familiar song: "This Land Is Your Land," page 20.[1]

B. Review, "The Night Is Serene," page 2.
(This song was presented to the class for the first time last week. Miss Jones expects the children to be able to sing the song this week without her help.)

[1] Harry R. Wilson et al., *Growing with Music,* Book 4 (Englewood Cliffs, N.J.: Prentice-Hall, Inc., 1963). All other song titles used in this chapter refer to the appropriate grade-level book of this series. Other available series may, of course, be used in a similar manner.

   C. "Scramble" the titles of the individual sections of Saint-Saëns' *Carnival of the Animals:*

Correct sequence	"Scrambled" order
Hens and Cocks	Turtles
Fleet-footed Animals	Long-Eared Personages
Turtles	The Elephant
The Elephant	Aquarium
Kangaroos	Hens and Cocks
Aquarium	Kangaroos
Long-Eared Personages	Fleet-footed Animals

   (Miss Jones' purpose is to see how well children can identify Saint-Saëns' musical "pictures" of the animals. She has chosen seven sections of the complete composition. She places the titles in "scrambled" order on the chalkboard and asks the boys and girls to list them in their correct order.)

   D. Sing "Marching to Pretoria," page 47.
   (Selected by Miss Jones because this is a familiar song that fourth-graders particularly enjoy.)

This is certainly not elaborate planning. To do any less would be improvisation. With considerable experience and a wealth of material at her finger-tips, Miss Jones might be able to do an acceptable job of improvising for a short time. But even for an experienced elementary music specialist to extemporize day after day produces a program without substance, without direction, and with little learning.

When Miss Jones enters Mrs. Susan Crandall's fourth-grade room with her carefully prepared lesson on *Carnival of the Animals,* she discovers that Mrs. Crandall has been anxiously awaiting her arrival.

"Miss Jones, we are so glad to see you. We need some help with the square dance that we are to perform at the school assembly next week." What does Miss Jones do? Of course, she postpones her planned presentation of *Carnival of the Animals.* She is happy to receive any specific request for assistance. She responds to Mrs. Crandall's request with alacrity and with enthusiasm.

Basically, Miss Jones' plans for a classroom visit have a beginning, e.g., a familiar song, a middle (the major topic or "heart" of the visit) and an end, e.g., a familiar song, a favorite recording. Within this basic framework, endless variations are possible. In many instances, Miss Jones plans the middle or "heart" of her visit carefully but varies both the beginning and end with each class.

This procedure is not offered as a definitive formula. There is no one best way to supervise elementary music just as there is no one best way to teach. The plan used by Miss Jones is one of many that could be followed. For her it is a good one. It is not the only one nor the "best" one.

Is it defensible for Miss Jones to use her plan in several classrooms?

Specifically, if she has a planned presentation for *Carnival of the Animals* for Mrs. Crandall's fourth-grade class, may she use the presentation with good professional conscience in other fourth-grade classes? One might hedge and equivocate in replying, but the answer is *yes*. A carefully planned presentation for two classes may be similar but it will never develop in exactly the same way. Plans for teaching may be systematic but learning cannot be systematized. The children's responses will vary widely from room to room and, for that matter, within one classroom. If the presentation is effective, there is no reason why it should not be repeated. It is far better to repeat an effective presentation several times than to have widely varied but indifferently planned and ineffective presentations in each classroom.

In practice, Miss Jones has discovered that it is a rare occasion when she is able to implement her presentation exactly as it was planned. Perhaps, for the first time, one of her musically-timid teachers is willing to lead the class in a familiar song while Miss Jones is in the room. Such an event warrants a complete departure from the planned offering. Perhaps both the children and the teacher request the repetition of an activity that was done several weeks ago that Miss Jones did not plan to do at all. Or a newly-mounted display of work on the chalkboard and tackboard may suggest a musical approach that will spark more interest than the planned activity. It is very easy to depart from a plan if there is a clue for another approach or another activity that may have more immediate value. However, it is very difficult to improvise a plan "on the spot."

As important as the plan is the necessity for recording in some way *what actually happened*. Marginal notes, checks for completed items, comments on a facing page—there are many possible "bookkeeping" systems. The actual visit and the planned visit must be seen "in parallel" if one is to evaluate effectively and to improve planning for future visits. A running log of supervisory visits can be an important instrument in the professional self-improvement of the elementary music consultant.

To exemplify some of the points that have been made, let us again examine Miss Jones' notebook to see the kind of planning she might make for one week of classroom visitation. At this particular time, Miss Jones' energies are focused on playing instruments at all levels in the elementary classroom.

In looking at these plans, we shall consider A as the introductory phase of the lesson and C as the concluding activity. B is the most important item of the presentation. We shall assume that A and C are familiar material that may be performed quickly and easily. B is either new material or familiar material that is being extended. Not all planned visits and, of course, not all actual visits will fall into this neat three-part arrangement. Sometimes, for example, B will provide its own natural conclusion. Or, because of the nature of B, an A may be unnecessary.

Let us examine Miss Jones' plans for one visit at each grade level:

November, first week.

Emphasis: playing classroom instruments.

Grade I

A. Sing "Nicholas Ned," page 48.[2]

B. "Play and Sing," page 40. Use for first experiences in playing rhythm instruments.

1. Clap steady *one-two* beat.

2. Sing verses for sticks, tone-block, triangle.

3. Play steady *one-two* beat with appropriate instrument.

C. Sing "All Night, All Day," page 9.

Grade II

A. Sing "The Clapping Land," page 28.

B. Sing "Birds Are Flying Homeward," page 119.

1. Show direction of melody with hand movements.

2. Play bell part on bells.

3. Play melody part on bells, accompaniment on autoharp.

C. Sing and play bell part for "Ah, Poor Bird," page 10.

Grade III

A. Sing and play "Oranges and Lemons," page 76.

B. "We Are Fine Musicians," page 82.

1. Play instruments as indicated in the text.

2. Sing song cumulative style at brisk tempo to encourage precise playing.

3. Ask students to make up other verses such as: "On the jingle bells we go ring-a-ling," "On the little drum we go boom, boom, boom."

C. Play the "Rhythm Round," page 141.

Grade IV

A. Sing "I'm Gonna Sing," page 1.

B. "In Bahia Town," page 69.

1. Learn melody.

2. Use bells (or song flutes in some classrooms) for the melody instrument part.

3. Play rhythm instruments as follows on the refrain:

[2] All page numbers and song titles refer to the appropriate grade level book in the *Growing with Music* series.

C. Sing and play "Fifty Stars," page 76.

Grade V

A. Sing "Stodala Pumpa," page 98.
B. "The Luau," page 122.
   1. Use melody bells and/or song flutes on descant.
   2. Use ukulele accompaniment in those rooms where ukuleles are available; otherwise, use autoharps.
   3. Make up and notate a percussive accompaniment.
C. Sing and play "Changing of the Guard," page 12, using the drum and triangle parts developed last week.

Grade VI

A. Sing "My Boat Is Sailing," page 146, with instrumental descant (bells or violin).
B. "Toraji," page 151.
   1. Point out that this is a pentatonic melody using five tones: C, D, F, G, and A.
   2. Make up ostinati on bells and/or piano.
   3. Play the accompaniments given in the student's book.
   4. Add a percussive accompaniment creating an "oriental" sound with such instruments as triangle, wood block, gong, etc. Use a different instrument on each of the three pulses of the following rhythmic pattern:

C. Sing "Dry Bones," page 148, with percussive accompaniment.

Organizing the Work

The visitation schedule of the elementary music consultant is of primary concern in organizing and carrying out her work. The number of schools assigned to her is something over which she generally has little control. A music specialist may work entirely at the elementary level or she may have a combined elementary-secondary responsibility. Usually her working schedule is established prior to her appointment. It is her responsibility, once she accepts her appointment, to work as effectively as possible within the assigned framework.

Miss Jones' working schedule is fairly typical of the consultant who works full time in the elementary program. She is assigned to four elementary schools. She works one full day in each of the two smaller schools and one and one-half days in the two larger schools.

Within each building, the visitation schedule of the consultant is the responsibility of the principal. In the Broadmoor Elementary School, Miss Jones' schedule is based on the premise that she can comfortably complete eight visits during the day. However, Miss Jones often makes as many as ten classroom visits or more when it becomes necessary for her to do so. Since the Broadmoor faculty includes twelve teachers, it is not possible for her to see every teacher during the one day she is assigned to work in the building. Both Mr. Hawkins and Miss Jones feel that thirty minutes is the minimum time to allow for a classroom visit and a brief conference.

Together with Mr. Hawkins and the total school faculty, Miss Jones organizes her time on a fixed schedule with those teachers who most need her help. Occasionally she combines two grades but, as a general rule, she works with one class in the regular classroom setting.

With six visits regularly scheduled each time that she is in the school, Miss Jones has time for two, three, or four visits that may be used in a more flexible manner. During this time she may "look in" on a teacher like Edith McElroy several times during the month. Mrs. McElroy requires little help but she is always happy to have Miss Jones visit. Or Mr. Hawkins may schedule occasional school-wide assembly sings. Or Miss Jones takes care of "on call" requests. Or she may use this time for curriculum development in a particular area. Or she may schedule needed conferences with individual teachers. Or she may use part of this time to direct the school chorus.

Miss Jones feels that in many ways the flexible portion of her schedule is most productive. She answers specific requests for help. Motivation on the part of both teachers and pupils is high and the chances for learning are good. Mr. Hawkins assists by relaying requests of teachers to Miss Jones. A "Music Help" request sheet on which teachers may indicate their needs is posted on the faculty bulletin board in the Broadmoor Elementary School.

A number of generalities are in order concerning the schedule of the elementary music consultant within the school building:

1. The schedule must be cooperatively set by the principal, his faculty, and the consultant.
2. A greater portion of the consultant's day should be definitely scheduled. If possible, it is highly desirable to schedule several visits on a flexible basis.
3. Teachers who need help most should be visited regularly.
4. Regardless of how proficient or self-sufficient an elementary teacher may be in music, she should be visited by the music consultant periodically.
5. As a general rule, the consultant should visit one class at a time in its regular classroom setting. Multi-class groupings are desirable from time to time but they should be the exception rather than the norm.
6. The consultant's schedule should be evaluated periodically. All concerned—the principal, the teachers, and the consultant—should have an opportunity to evaluate.
7. Provision should be made for in-service group meetings with teachers in addition to visits in the classroom.

8. It is important to bear in mind that the supervisory schedule of the consultant is superimposed on the daily schedule of the school. Adjustments must be made by the consultant just as the classroom teacher makes adjustments in her classroom schedule.

9. When a fixed schedule is established, it is important for the consultant to adhere to it as closely as possible. Too often the inexperienced consultant in her zeal to visit as many rooms as possible will schedule her visits so closely that there is inadequate time for either classroom work or conferences.

10. Details such as developing an efficient movement pattern for the consultant from room to room can best be worked out by the principal. Refinements and adjustments will be made as the schedule is carried out.

11. There is no one schedule for an elementary music consultant within the school that has proved to be "the best way." The general observations made here must be adapted to each particular school situation.

Criteria for establishing a working schedule for the elementary music specialist have not been clearly defined. It would be reassuring if every consultant were able to visit and work with each teacher in her own classroom at least once a week. A music program of substance, worth, and integrity may be developed under such a minimal arrangement. But what if the consultant does not have such a minimal working situation? Like any professional, she does the very best she can. Multi-class groupings, "skipping" the rooms of teachers who have some degree of musical independence, eliminating conference periods, rest periods, and reducing her lunch hour is the rule rather than the exception for the music consultant.

At the same time, in all candor, it must be recognized that a desirable schedule in and of itself guarantees one very little. The musicianship and personality of the consultant are of far greater importance. Many imaginative, resourceful consultants accomplish miracles within a schedule that, on the surface, appears to be impossible. The attitude of the principal toward music education, the rapport between consultant and teachers, the quality and quantity of instructional materials all have important influences on the caliber of instruction in music.

Although our emphasis in this chapter has been on planning and scheduling, there are other factors that need to be taken into consideration in terms of program organization:

1. A good part of the consultant's ability to organize and carry out the program successfully is dependent on her professional training and her continuing efforts in professional improvement. Keeping informed of new procedures and implementing them is one of her important functions.

2. Periodic demonstrations for teachers are desirable. A verbal description of a given procedure is not nearly so effective as seeing it in operation with boys and girls.

3. Inter-visitations can be important in-service functions. For many teachers, the observation of a colleague in action is much more convincing than seeing the specialist demonstrating the same procedure.

4. The cooperative preparation of a curriculum guide in music by the elementary teachers and music consultants does much to organize and activate a program.

5. Periodic mimeographed suggestions to teachers or descriptions of effective teaching practices are effective in-service instruments. Promising practices should be shared.

6. The willingness of the elementary music consultant to participate in action research can do much not only to improve the local program but the entire field of elementary music. There is a great need for thorough research in elementary music education.

7. One of the very best ways to refine both planning and organization is through a process of continuing evaluation. The consultant must evaluate daily. In addition, it is strongly recommended that periodic evaluations be made by all concerned: teachers, principals, consultants, supervisors, administrators, and patrons.

Summary

In this chapter we have set forth suggested procedures for translating broad generalizations and continuing aims into the day-by-day work of the elementary music consultant. Both long-range and short-range planning are necessary. The consultant must first perceive her task as an entity. In addition, she must be able to relate the elementary music program to the total school program.

Keeping these broad concepts in mind, a logical next step is to consider annual planning. The consultant should have definite objectives in mind for the year's work. It is necessary that they be defined clearly enough so that they may be expressed in written form. Annual plans will vary from year to year depending on the current status of the program.

Many different approaches may be made to monthly planning. Like annual planning, the goals must be both specific and flexible. Several approaches were developed: emphasizing approaches to musical understanding, and considering the musical learnings themselves as points of emphasis. Others suggested were: implementing basic concepts from professional literature, integrating the study of music with other areas of the elementary curriculum, and relating the objectives of music education to a system-wide program of curriculum improvement. There is no one formula that will fit all situations.

In her weekly planning, the consultant needs to avoid the extremes of inadequate planning and over-planning. Suggestions were presented in sample plans for grades one through six. In essence, Miss Jones carefully plans for the "heart" of each supervisory visit. Although her visits are always pre-planned, Miss Jones is quick to seize on requests of teachers and emerging interests of children. She has discovered it is very easy to depart from a pre-conceived plan while it is very difficult to improvise a plan "on the spot."

In organizing her work, the consultant usually has little control over her building schedule. Within the school, her working schedule is the primary responsibility of the elementary principal. All or most of her time is allocated on a "fixed schedule," although it is desirable to have some time set aside for "on call" services.

Definite criteria for establishing the consultant's schedule within a school have yet to be made. It is recommended, as a minimum goal, that the consultant be able to work with each teacher in her own classroom at least once each week. It is recognized, however, that the musicianship, the personality, and the resourcefulness of the consultant are the most important factors in developing an effective supervisory program in the elementary school.

Questions for Discussion

1. List five or six points that would give direction to a year's planning for the elementary music consultant.
2. Several possibilities have been given in this chapter for developing monthly plans. Suggest others.
3. Develop a list of five or six objectives for one month of a consultant's work.
4. What are some dangers of over-planning? of under-planning?
5. Develop a plan for one classroom visit.
6. Discuss the "beginning-middle-end" format suggested for a supervisory visit.
7. Develop one plan for each of the elementary grades. Use available music series as references.
8. What is your reaction to using the same basic plan in several classrooms?
9. Suggest some practical procedures for the consultant to record what actually happened during the classroom visit.
10. How many supervisory visits do you believe that a music consultant should make in one day? Assuming that the school begins at 8:30 A.M. and dismisses at 3:30 P.M., draw up a schedule for the consultant.

Part Three

The Curriculum Team

10

The Role of
the Elementary Teacher

The teaching of music in the elementary school is a cooperative venture involving the efforts of teacher, specialist, and principal. Others are also engaged, but these are the people most directly concerned. In this section, we shift our focus from the elementary music specialist to the elementary teacher, the principal, the supervisor, and the administrator. The cooperative approach cannot be broken down into isolated responsibilities but the various roles can be better understood if each is considered in turn.

In this chapter we are primarily concerned with the elementary teacher. She is the central figure in the elementary music teaching program. Today most of the music instruction in American schools at the elementary level is carried on by the elementary teacher with varying degrees of help and guidance from the music specialist. In the majority of schools, either the elementary teacher accepts the responsibility for teaching music or there is no program.

It is rarely possible for a school board to finance a program of elementary music that is taught exclusively by specialists. Even more important, there is a growing realization among general educators and music educators that a cooperative approach utilizing the resources and talents of the classroom teacher and the specialist is more productive.

The resistance that some teachers have to teaching music is understandable. The elementary teacher is expected to have proficiency in many areas. It is not uncommon for an otherwise competent teacher to feel quite at a loss in providing musical experiences for boys and girls.

However, it is quite remarkable how much the musically timid teacher can accomplish with the help of a sympathetic and resourceful music consultant. In teaching music in the elementary school, the classroom teacher's responsibility is to set the stage for learning. If the activity is sufficiently provocative, the children will do a very great deal on their own initiative.

The classroom teacher's unique specialty is that she knows children well at a given chronological level. Mrs. Susan Crandall knows each of her fourth-grade children as individuals. She is an expert in the knowledge of nine-year-olds in general and her children in particular. Even though she may not be as secure in teaching music as she would like to be, she is perfectly within her rights to challenge the music consultant when she feels that a suggested musical learning is inappropriate for the developmental level of her boys and girls.

The great majority of elementary teachers with rudimentary college preparation in music education can become quite proficient with the help of an effective music consultant. Although the consultant is interested in a broad gamut of activities that include singing, playing, listening, moving, creating, and reading, she should develop these activities by catering to the strengths and interests of each teacher with whom she works. For example, Miss Mary Armstrong frankly admits that she is not too enthusiastic about any music teaching. However, she is willing to make an effort to provide listening experiences for her sixth-grade children. Rather than indicate that there are many more important projects that have a greater priority, Miss Carol Jones does all she can to encourage and develop this evidenced interest. She builds from this point.

If Miss Edna Allen prefers to work primarily with rhythms and dances in her first-grade class, Miss Jones reinforces and supports her. The insecure teacher should not be overwhelmed by the organization and structure of the total music program in all of its aspects. Her great need is to achieve a measure of success in at least one approach. The elementary teacher needs a feeling of success in one phase of teaching music before she will attempt other activities.

Attitude

More than any other single factor, the *attitude* of the elementary teacher toward music will determine the effectiveness of the program in her classroom. This involves not only her attitude as a teacher of music but also as an individual responding to music in everyday life.

Mrs. Susan Crandall is interested in music. She seeks out opportunities to hear music and she includes some music-making in her leisure hours. The chances for her offering music in her fourth-grade class are good.

Miss Armstrong feels that music is something to be tolerated if one has nothing better to do. She has had little contact with music beyond the required semester in her undergraduate education. Her own experience in music as a student in public school was extremely limited. She does not now participate in any music activity nor does she attend concerts. The chances for her offering vital, meaningful experiences in her classroom are not very good.

Response to music is such a highly personalized affair that it is impossible to separate the teacher from the person. If a teacher herself is quite unresponsive to music, it would be most surprising to find a comprehensive, vital program of music education in her classroom.

Those values that we emphasize in our own lives we hope to see valued by others. Mrs. Crandall, to whom music is of great worth, is concerned that her boys and girls also become familiar with the expressive language of music. Although Miss Armstrong does not deliberately withhold music experiences from her children, there is a minimal level of music activity in her classroom.

The crucial importance of teacher attitude suggests many things. For one, it indicates very clearly that music education classes for teachers at the college level must do more than "cover the ground." They must be musically satisfying and stimulating. In-service group work must not only be concerned with skills and techniques, but also must provide opportunities for the musical growth of the teacher.

For the teacher who has had limited experiences in music, perhaps the best advice the elementary music consultant can give is to suggest that she become actively involved in some kind of music making. Singing in a church choir, attending local community concerts, enrolling in a group piano class, participating in a summer music education workshop, taking additional college music courses as a part of her master's degree program are examples of the kinds of activities that can do much to increase a teacher's understanding of music. The constant aim of the elementary music consultant should be to increase the musicality of each teacher she serves.

The members of the faculty of a typical elementary school will have varying attitudes toward music as well as different abilities to teach music. A very few teachers will be highly musical. They will need little or no help from the consultant except for a word of encouragement and appreciation. A very few teachers will be so disinterested or resistant that very little music teaching will go on in their classes except when the consultant is there. However, the great majority of faculty members are willing to make an honest attempt to teach music if they are given periodic, adequate help from a resourceful consultant.

With a positive attitude toward music as a person and as a teacher, the acceptance of responsibility to teach music is no problem. Once a classroom teacher is convinced as to the *why* of teaching music, the *how* becomes quite clear. The capable elementary teacher *wants* to teach music. In fact, she would be quite indignant if it were suggested that she not do so. An "outstanding" elementary teacher will also do a better-than-average job of teaching music.

With a favorable point of view and expert consultant help, it is quite possible for the elementary teacher to organize musical learnings that will not only be of great benefit to her children but will bring teaching rewards to herself.

Resources Available to the Teacher

Perhaps the most important resources available to the teacher are her background, training, and experience as a teacher of all elementary subjects. Although she may feel inadequate in terms of technical preparation in music, the experienced teacher has a sensitivity to the kinds of musical experiences that her children will respond to positively.

The knowledgeable music consultant will encourage the elementary teacher to "play her hunches" in regard to music offerings. The elementary teacher should think of music making in her classroom neither as a smoothly planned rehearsal nor as a highly skilled presentation but rather as an everyday classroom experience. The procedure used in teaching a song is of less consequence than the fact that her children sing. Many teachers begin a song without preliminaries. By their manner and their facial expression they literally invite children to "join in."

It is true that music is an involved and highly technical language, but it is also true that music makes a direct emotional impact that transcends the technicalities involved.

Another important resource to the teacher is the children in her class who are able to assume leadership roles in music activities. In the upper grades, particularly, students who are studying privately can be of help in interpreting notation, explaining musical terms, and, perhaps, providing accompaniments. Some children will be pleased to be invited to lead the class in a favorite song.

Students in the upper grades who take private piano lessons are rarely called on except to play a solo at a school assembly. The private teacher would be delighted to teach accompaniments for some of the songs used in the classroom if she were given the opportunity to do so. Fledgling pianists would profit greatly from the experience. The classroom music activities would be enriched.

It is rather surprising how often resource help of this kind is ignored even when it is badly needed. It is a resourceful teacher who invites sixth graders who have been experimenting with ukuleles in their after-school get-togethers to provide accompaniments for class singing.

Oftentimes the material resources at the disposal of the elementary teacher are not fully used. Nearly every classroom is furnished with one of the basic music series that has been especially designed for use in the elementary school. It is most discouraging to discover how many copies of the well-prepared teacher's manual designed to accompany these books go begging for use! Not only do these manuals contain the necessary accompaniments but practical teaching procedures for each song are outlined. They suggest one or more activities that may be used to highlight important musical learnings or to relate this song with other classroom undertakings.

If the elementary teacher is to do a creditable job of teaching music she must plan for it just as she does for any other subject. Although it would be unrealistic to expect her to plan on the same detailed basis that we have suggested for the specialist, she can do some very satisfactory preparation if she will begin with the instructions in the teacher's manual for her basic music textbook.

Each of the current music series has recordings that parallel the songs in the student's book. If the teacher is unable to read notes, she may teach a song to her children by using these related recordings. In addition to using the recordings for teaching songs, they may also be used for accompaniments, listening, bodily movement, dramatizations, playing instruments, and creative activities.

There are many other audio-visual helps. Movies and film-strips are most effective. Radio broadcasts have long been used in elementary music and teaching by television is particularly appropriate for music instruction. Each year more and more audio-visual aids are developed to assist the classroom teacher in her music program.

Cooperative Relations with the Music Consultant

The point has been made several times that the elementary teacher is a key person in the elementary music program. However, most teachers are quite dependent on the guidance and help of the consultant. It is important that the teacher regard the consultant primarily as a helping teacher, and as a teacher of children only secondarily. The consultant cannot possibly function as the direct teacher of music in most American schools. This is true for a number of obvious reasons.

First, the consultant cannot visit each classroom often enough to provide adequate, direct teaching. A once-a-week visit may be adequate in terms of consultant help for the teacher; however, a weekly visit by the consultant is woefully inadequate if this is the only instruction in music that boys and girls receive.

The elementary teacher is able to teach music in a flexible, functional manner that is impossible for the consultant to duplicate. Unfortunately, children's readiness for music instruction does not always coincide with the visit of the consultant.

Second, the consultant cannot come to know individual children well enough to adapt to each one's unique potentialities or to draw on each one for his special contribution. When the consultant speaks to the teacher she refers to the class as *"your* children," never "my children."

Third, the consultant, although she is responsible for overall planning in terms of long-range musical goals, cannot possibly be as well informed as the teacher with regard to how to best relate music to the total instructional program. The tutorial music supervisor who delegates specific responsibilities to the teachers and expects them carried out to the letter belongs to a past era. Many significant developments in music education have come about from the skillfulness and resourcefulness of the elementary teacher.

The elementary teacher expects to be a co-worker with the consultant. Her ideas and goals are at least as worthy as those advocated by the consultant. What most elementary teachers want from the specialist is guidance and help in translating a desired program into action. They expect her to keep them informed as to procedures, classroom instruments, recordings, and other instructional materials. They hope for encouragement, advice, and stimulation. Perhaps more than anything else, they want some good, practical, down-to-earth ideas as to how *they* can bring music to their boys and girls.

The primary responsibility for carrying on the music program is that of the elementary teacher. Everything the music consultant does must be oriented toward the basic goal of helping classroom teachers become more effective in teaching music. This is the consultant's primary reason for being.

Principles of Learning

Reassuring to teachers, principals, and supervisors alike is the fact that the principles of learning apply to the teaching of music as to any other area of the curriculum. The experienced principal applies the same criteria in evaluating a learning situation in music as he does in appraising the teaching of language arts. The elementary teacher decides whether a music activity is appropriate and significant on the same basis that she evaluates her other work.

In music teaching, as in other teaching, we recognize:

1. that learning is an active process.
2. that learnings are more apt to happen when organized around a central idea.

3. that learnings must be presented with a concern for the developmental readiness of boys and girls.

4. that learning is continuous.

5. that the learning must have recognizable value or purpose for the learner.

6. that learning proceeds best when the learner can see results.

7. that the degree of learning is directly affected by the aspiration level of the student.

8. that learnings must take into account individual differences.

9. that learnings must be satisfying experiences, that success must be achieved more often than failure.

10. that repetition is essential but that mechanical drill itself will not produce learning.

11. that spaced experiences over a period of time are more productive than compressed experiences.

12. that learning is a creative process of inquiring, discovering, and perceiving.

Whatever the teacher may lack in terms of a theoretical understanding of music, she can draw on her total teaching experience for the organization and presentation of musical learnings. With a positive point of view toward music teaching and with the continuing assistance of the consultant, she can bring satisfying musical experiences to her boys and girls.

In-service Education

Most of the in-service education for teachers is carried on in the classroom during the supervisory visit of the consultant. It should be obvious that it is absolutely essential that the teacher remain during the entire time that the consultant is in the classroom.

Anyone in elementary education will agree that the elementary teacher has a very full day and that she is entitled to a "break" as much as any worker in any other field of endeavor. However, if the elementary music consultant is looked upon as a helping, resource teacher whose mission is to improve the musicality of teachers, it is imperative that the teacher not only remain but that she also actively participate. It is ridiculous to employ a helping teacher in music when the teacher she is supposed to help is not physically present when she is at work!

The whole in-service approach becomes impossible when the visit of the elementary music consultant is looked upon only as a welcome respite for the teacher. Although the consultant may be working with the children, her efforts are directed toward the musical growth of the teacher as well.

Organized teacher-study groups represent another important in-service activity. More often than not, these groups are organized on a voluntary basis. In some systems, however, they are compulsory.

How the in-service groups are organized is a matter of secondary importance. What is important is that teachers participate. There are many topics to be discussed, ideas to be exchanged, problems to be solved, procedures to be demonstrated, and skills to be acquired that are impossible to consider when children are present. The in-service group provides the elementary teacher with an opportunity to work on specific things she may apply immediately. Most elementary teachers are more interested in acquiring specific learnings and skills than they are in dealing in abstractions or generalizations. They want to learn how to use the school's record library. They want to learn to play the autoharp or the recorder or resonator bells. They want to know what they are supposed to teach about notation at their grade level.

In-service study groups should contribute to the musicality of each teacher. The skills, knowledge, and techniques acquired should make her less reliant on the help of the specialist. To push the point to an ultimate ideal, the in-service groups should be so successful over an extended period of time that experienced elementary teachers would be able to teach without specialist assistance. Although this idealistic goal can never be achieved for all teachers, it points out very clearly the direction that in-service activities should take.

For example, Miss Carol Jones organizes an in-service group centering on class piano. The needs and interests of elementary teachers are uppermost in Miss Jones' mind. Her objective, in one year of work, is to make it possible for elementary teachers to play the single line melodies of the songs in their grade-level books and to improvise "block chord" accompaniments. With this rudimentary keyboard background, Miss Jones knows that elementary teachers can be much more independent in planning and carrying out their music instruction. Although she uses class piano as a point of departure, Miss Jones' primary aim is to develop the musicality of each teacher.

In-service group members will learn much from each other. The consultant, although she may be the recognized leader, should not completely dominate the proceedings. Many of the favorite songs and teaching procedures that are widely used by elementary teachers have been acquired from other elementary teachers. Too often there is a marked difference between the activities that the consultant introduces during her periodic visits and the activities that teachers actually use. Rather than being alarmed when she first discovers this, the consultant should attempt to find out the kinds of things that teachers consider to be functional.

Mrs. Crandall, a fourth-grade teacher with twenty-five years of successful experience, will certainly have a few suggestions when the new teacher asks her if she knows any good Halloween songs. In one school district, a successful technique for teaching a listening lesson on Saint-Saëns' "Carnival of the Animals" was passed from teacher to teacher. Some of the very best and widely used teaching procedures in elementary music education have been developed by creative, resourceful elementary teachers.

Once she is accepted and respected by elementary teachers, the elementary music consultant can provide a valuable service by collecting favorite songs, recordings, procedures, and ideas that have been used for many years by certain teachers and passing them along, with proper credits, to other interested teachers. A mimeographed singing game that is distributed to primary teachers with the note, "As used in Miss Allen's first grade, Broadmoor Elementary School," can do much for improving teaching as well as teacher morale.

Elementary teachers should realize that music activities must be sufficiently varied so that every child may participate effectively in music making. Activities should be arranged so that immediate success is possible. In addition, they must be arranged sequentially so that progress is made to deeper and fuller responsiveness.

The elementary teacher is able, more than any other person, to see to it that music can be purposeful and meaningful within the framework of the daily classroom schedule. Music should be taught as a significant learning in its own right. It should also be correlated with other subjects when it is appropriate to do so.

Remember that the new teacher is not completely equipped to teach music even if she is certified to do so under state requirements. The elementary teacher should, with help and guidance, grow each year in her ability to teach music just as she improves in her ability to teach other subjects. She must be willing, literally, to learn along with her children. She should strive for a better program in music each year that she teaches. Given the necessary consultant help, the basic instructional materials, and adequate in-service education, the elementary teacher will come to be as successful in music teaching as she is in language arts or any other area.

The elementary teacher who does an effective job of teaching music in her classroom:

1. accepts her responsibility to provide music instruction.
2. welcomes the help provided by the consultant.
3. remains in the classroom and actively participates during the consultant's visit.
4. plans cooperatively with the consultant, the principal, and administrators.
5. keeps the consultant informed as to her plans, her needs, and her interests.
6. provides an atmosphere in which children can grow musically.
7. indicates by her attitude her enthusiasm for music.
8. values music in her personal life.
9. sees the value of music education for boys and girls.
10. plans her music instruction.
11. draws on her specialized knowledge of children in providing music experiences.

12. provides necessary instructional materials.
13. makes wise use of instruments, equipment, and materials.
14. makes use of the human resources in her classroom.
15. makes use of musical resources in the community.
16. applies the principles of learning in evaluating music instruction.
17. is receptive to new ideas and new procedures.
18. shares effective teaching procedures with others.
19. welcomes the opportunity to participate in in-service groups.
20. keeps parents informed of their child's growth in music.

Summary

The elementary teacher has the central role in the elementary music teaching program. In most American schools she is responsible for carrying on the music program with the help and guidance of the music consultant.

The teacher has specialized knowledge in knowing children well at a given chronological level. Therefore, she has much to offer in cooperative planning with the consultant. This is true even though her theoretical knowledge of music may be limited.

Perhaps the most important single factor that will determine the success of her music instruction is her personal attitude toward music. If music is important in her everyday living she will recognize the importance of music education for her boys and girls. With a positive attitude, her success in teaching music to her boys and girls is virtually assured.

In a typical elementary school faculty, a few teachers will be so musically independent as to require little help from the music consultant. A very few teachers will be so disinterested or resistant that the consultant must do most of the direct teaching. However, the great majority of teachers can satisfactorily handle their music teaching if given adequate, periodic consultant help.

The teacher has many resources available to her in the classroom. Her own broad teaching experience is of great help in planning music experiences. Abilities of children who can assume leadership roles in music should be utilized. Available materials of instruction should be used effectively.

The elementary teacher should expect the music consultant to be a co-worker. She should not hesitate to advance her own ideas in the cooperative planning sessions. It is vital that she willingly accept her responsibility as the person who is most influential in determining the quality of instruction in her classroom.

The principles of learning apply to music as they do to any subject area. They should be used in evaluating and improving music offerings.

An important in-service activity is professional group study. In-service groups provide specific, functional skills that the teacher can apply at once to her program of instruction. It is important to remember that teachers learn from other teachers as well as from the music consultant. The consultant should not attempt to dominate the in-service group. The elementary teacher should be receptive to new ideas. She should also be willing to share her own successful teaching procedures with others.

Elementary teachers recognize that music should be taught as a significant learning in its own right. It should also be correlated with other subjects when appropriate. Few beginning teachers are completely prepared to teach music. The new teacher should be willing to learn along with her children. She will improve in her ability to teach music as she does in teaching other subjects.

Questions for Discussion

1. What are some of the more common reasons for a teacher's resistance to teaching music in her classes?
2. In what sense is the elementary teacher a specialist?
3. Discuss this statement: "More than any other factor, the attitude of the elementary teacher toward music will determine the effectiveness of the music program in her classroom."
4. What are some of the human and material resources available as helps to music teaching for the elementary teacher?
5. Is it possible for the principal who has had a limited background in music education to supervise the program of music in his school? Why?
6. What are some important considerations to bear in mind in planning for in-service work?
7. What is the consultant's leadership role in the in-service study group?
8. As a music consultant, what advice would you give to the new, inexperienced elementary teacher who feels that she is not equipped to teach music?
9. As a music consultant, what would you do in the case of the mature, experienced teacher who is resistant to teaching music in her classroom?
10. Why is the matter of the teacher's valuation of music in her own personal life so important in her music teaching?

11

*The Role of
the Elementary Principal*

The principal is not only the professional leader in his school but he plays an important leadership role in the community. He is recognized as the administrator as well as the supervisor of instruction in his building. He is regarded as an educational leader in curriculum development. He is expected to interpret the principles of learning to patrons and he is considered to be an expert in the area of child development.

Not only is he the leading spokesman for his school in the community but, in turn, he is sensitive to the expectations and aspirations that the community has for its children. More than anyone else, he sets the "tone" of the educational program in his school.

Supervising the Program

The elementary principal supervises and administers the music program as he does other phases of the educational endeavor. Just as the elementary teacher's attitude toward music is an important factor in determining the calibre of her music instruction, so does the principal's evaluation of music determine his estimate of the role of music in elementary education.

The principal establishes a climate for learning because of the kind of person he is, the depth of his understandings, the quality of his thinking, and the clarity of his perceptions. Whether he regards music as significant or trivial will have a great deal to do with the status of music in his school.

Perhaps the most positive influence the principal can bring to bear is his *expectation* that each elementary teacher is responsible for teaching music. If his teachers know he expects this, music will be included in the daily schedule. It may vary in quantity and quality, but it will be there.

However, if he indicates directly or indirectly that "it's all right with me if you do and all right with me if you don't," his teachers will react accordingly. The indifference of a principal as to whether music is or is not included in the daily schedule can negate the combined efforts of teachers and consultants.

The principal should recognize music for its unique contribution to the aesthetic development of children. Satisfying aesthetic experiences are sought by every child in every culture on this earth. Although the entertainment and recreational values of music are not to be denied, it is hoped that the principal will not relegate the study of music to a "fun" status equivalent to watching the amateur magician's performance at the school carnival.

The elementary principal supervises the music program in a number of ways.

He supervises teachers through classroom visits. As he makes supervisory visits to classrooms he evaluates music intruction as he does other instruction. He applies the same criteria in appraising teaching effectiveness and he does everything he can to activate or stimulate further improvement. He helps each teacher realize that she has something constructive to offer in the way of singing, playing, listening, or moving to music. He indicates his interest in the work being done. When he enters the classroom during "music time" he does not encourage the teacher to "shift gears" so that he may observe some more "worthwhile" undertaking. He indicates to both the teacher and the children that their music work is significant and that he supports what they are doing.

The understanding principal realizes some of the reasons why teachers may feel insecure in their ability to teach music. Some have had only a minimal preparation as elementary education majors. It is possible that a few may have had no preparation in music whatsoever.

Too many of our present elementary teachers have had limited exposure to music in their own public school experience as students. The concept of a vital, stimulating school music program is unknown to them. Some teachers are of the opinion that music is a field best left to highly skilled practitioners. Regardless of continued reassurances, they consider themselves unqualified to teach music.

Some teachers may hold life-long resentment toward music because of unpleasant personal experiences. It is not unusual to discover that a resistant teacher was a "blackbird" in the second grade and that she was asked to sit and listen while the "bluebirds" sang.

Deep-seated resentment such as this is difficult to remove. The principal needs to understand his teachers and their problems to the same extent that the teacher attempts to know her children. If principals and music consultants are aware of some of the reasons for resistance on the part of teachers they may better plan ways of working with them in the classroom.

The principal supervises the work of the elementary music consultant. Unfortunately, in far too many cases, the elementary music consultant is something of a problem for the principal. It is possible that a specialist was employed because of community interests and demands. She is sent to the school with the administrator telling the principal in effect, "We are sending Miss Smith to your school one day each week to help you with your music program. We're not quite sure how she should function, but we're sure you can keep her busy."

Robert Hawkins, principal at Broadmoor Elementary School, schedules the visits of Miss Carol Jones to best serve the needs, abilities, and limitations of his teachers as he sees them. With a faculty of twelve, Miss Jones cannot visit each classroom every week. She and Mr. Hawkins have agreed not to schedule more than eight consultant visits per day.

The problem is put to the faculty for their consideration. After some discussion, it is agreed that teachers like Mrs. Crandall, who is skilled in teaching music, need not be visited as often as Miss Armstrong, who feels inadequate in music. With the faculty concurring, Miss Jones visits six classrooms on a definite schedule and "floats" on an on-call basis during the other two half-hour visitation periods. Miss Jones' schedule is not inflexible. It is adjusted frequently to meet changing needs.

This hypothetical situation is not applicable to every school. Yet certain generalizations may be drawn:

1. The schedule of the elementary music consultant should be prepared cooperatively by teachers, the principal, and the consultant. All who are affected by the schedule should be involved in the planning.
2. The greater part of the consultant's time should be definitely scheduled. Ideally, some "on call" time should be available for special requests.
3. The schedule should not remain constant. There is a need for re-evaluation in consideration of individual teachers gaining greater competencies, new projects that are inaugurated, changes in teaching personnel, and the like.
4. To divide the consultant's time for visiting each classroom on a mathematically equal basis is not the most effective way to arrange her schedule.
5. Consideration is given to in-service group work as well as to scheduled visits in the classroom.

The experienced principal realizes that he has a special problem when the elementary music consultant is new to teaching. Fresh from college, she finds herself in the rather presumptuous position of giving counsel and advice to experienced teachers, some of whom have been teaching more years than she has lived. The principal should help in every way he can to further her acceptance. The young, inexperienced specialist who is serving as a consultant to an experienced faculty needs special encouragement, advice, and support from her principal.

If instrumental music is included in the elementary program, *the principal also supervises the work of the instrumental teacher.* The problem here is somewhat different. First, the instrumental music person is *the* teacher. He is not working in a consultant capacity. Secondly, he takes youngsters *out* of the classroom situation rather than working *within* it. And, thirdly, a special space or rehearsal area is required.

However, the same basic supervisory principles apply. The principal will probably need to take more direct responsibility in organizing a schedule for the instrumental teacher, but he should consult with all concerned. The principal realizes that there is a double problem in scheduling instrumental music: (1) to disrupt classroom activities as little as possible, and (2) to make it possible for the instrumental teacher to offer the best possible instructional program within the time limitations.

The usual practice is to provide one or two full group rehearsals weekly in addition to some type of instrument class for each student. The principal seeks the opinion of the instrumental teacher as to what he would like to have in terms of an ideal schedule. It may be necessary for the principal to adapt and modify his requests to develop a practical, functional schedule for instrumental instruction.

The principal is in an advantageous position to promote a close working relationship between the elementary music specialist and the elementary instrumental music teacher. Instrumental students who are proficient enough to do so should be encouraged to perform in the classroom when it is appropriate.

Instrumental music teachers are often ambitious to develop a program quickly. Although the principal welcomes the instrumental teacher's zeal, it is his responsibility to see that the instrumental schedule is carried on in a manner consistent with the aims of the total school program.

The principal is concerned with improving instruction. The principal, like some teachers, may feel inadequate about his technical proficiency in music. However, he understands the broad aims of the music program and their relationship to educational objectives. The principal has frequent conferences with the elementary music consultant as to how the program may be improved.

Specifically, the principal may be helpful by encouraging experimentation and creativity. Teachers should be willing to "try their wings" with the understanding that failures will not bring censure. Creative opportunities in music teaching are great because of the nature of music itself and because music does not have definitely prescribed grade level minimums. The teacher has much latitude in exploring creative opportunities in music.

The principal can bring about instructional improvement by making it clear that the elementary teacher is expected to remain in the room during the consultant's visit. He also insists that music instruction be offered on those days when Miss Jones is not in the building.

One of the very best ways the principal can bring about improvement in music instruction is to coordinate and, if necessary, *to initiate* a program of in-service group study for teachers. Normally, Miss Jones would be the person to conduct these meetings but the special skills of individual teachers, other music consultants in the school system, and resource help in the community should be utilized as necessary.

With the many concerns that a school faculty has for improvement in all instructional areas, it is neither expected nor desirable that in-service group meetings in music go on all of the time. However, in considering instructional practices that need improving, Mr. Hawkins takes into account the necessity for improving instruction in music as he does for other areas of the curriculum.

One promising practice for in-service study is to involve elementary teachers in curriculum building. It is desirable to prepare a curriculum guide for an individual school even though there may be one for the state or the school system. Teachers will find this a stimulating project. It will also open the door for other in-service work.

Other in-service activities that the principal may consider include:

1. Scheduling music workshops.
2. Planning inter-visitation for teachers to other classrooms.
3. Arranging for demonstration teaching by the consultant or other resource persons.
4. Organizing study committees concerned with curriculum building and instructional improvement.
5. Selecting and evaluating materials.
6. Presenting occasional performances by visiting music groups.
7. Evaluating the music program.

The supervision of instruction is the most important contribution the principal can make toward the primary goal of the school—providing optimum educational experiences for boys and girls. The principal is an effective supervisor to the extent that he recognizes and fulfills this basic obligation.

Administering the Program

The principal's primary administrative responsibility with regard to music is to establish clearly the working role of the elementary music specialist. A lack of clarification of this role creates much misunderstanding.

Simply put, it comes to this: is the elementary specialist the music teacher, that is, one who does all or nearly all of the direct teaching; or, is her responsibility one of helping, guiding, and working with teachers as a music consultant?

It is important that the specialist and the teachers know just what the policy is for their school.

Mr. Hawkins, in accordance with the policy established in the Central City Schools, sees Miss Jones as a helping, consulting teacher. Miss Jones understood this to be her role at the time of her employment. In faculty meetings and in individual conferences, Mr. Hawkins clarifies Miss Jones' role. He leads professional discussions on the cooperative working relationship between the consultant and teachers. He helps teachers and the consultant define their responsibilities. He takes special care to indoctrinate new teachers. He takes every opportunity to dispel the notion that Miss Jones is *the* teacher of music, that is, the *only* person who teaches music at Broadmoor Elementary School.

As the administrator of his school, the principal does all within his power to secure and maintain adequate consultant help for his teachers. When there is a possibility of curtailing the music resource staff because of budgetary limitations, he represents his needs to the superintendent on the basis of his supervisory observations and the expressed wishes of his faculty.

In addition to the scheduled visits of Miss Jones, Mr. Hawkins also makes requests for supervisory assistance to the central office staff. Some of these requests are for help in music. Mr. Hughes, the Supervisor of Music, is a frequently invited visitor to Broadmoor School. He serves as an observer, a consultant, an in-service leader, and an advisor to the principal.

Mr. Hawkins discusses the music program as it relates to the total program with other principals, general supervisors, the director of instruction, and the superintendent. Although he is a competent principal with many years of successful experience, Mr. Hawkins solicits the advice and guidance of others in the system who are in a position to effect improvement in music education.

Another important administrative responsibility for the principal is the provision of adequate materials of instruction. In many school systems, an overall allotment for instructional materials is made to each school on the basis of pupil enrollment. The principal is usually the person who has the final responsibility in making judgments as to which requested items will be purchased.

He provides a music text for every child in the school. He sees to it that the accompanying teacher's manual is made available to each teacher.

He provides a complete set of the related recordings that accompany the basic series. In addition, he attempts to maintain a school library of basic recordings especially designed for elementary use. Supplementary recordings are purchased with his approval on the request of teachers and the consultant.

He provides such classroom instruments as rhythm instruments, resonator bells, xylophones, and autoharps. He realizes that a good quality record player is needed in every classroom. He understands that there must be at least one good piano in the school. Several pianos are desirable including one or two equipped with large rollers to facilitate movement from room to room. He sees to it that pianos are properly maintained and tuned periodically.

Books on music for reference purposes and general reading are found in the central school library or in individual classrooms. Music biographies, histories, dictionaries, as well as books on opera and the orchestra are included. All of these books are written for the elementary school child.

In addition, special music is needed for such groups as the elementary choir and the instrumental ensemble. If instrumental music is offered, there is a necessity to provide some of the instruments. They must be stored and cared for properly.

Interpreting the Program

The principal interprets the music program to the community in many ways. In his public relations, he emphasizes music's contribution to aesthetic development. He is careful not to over-emphasize public performance. The well-being of boys and girls is even more important than entertaining patrons or creating a desirable public relations "image." The elementary school cannot compete with the world of professional entertainment. Although a principal has many duties, being an impresario is not one of them.

Whenever possible, at P.T.A. meetings or at such activities as go-to-school-night, the principal and teachers acquaint parents with everyday classroom activities. A demonstration at P.T.A., for example, of how third-grade students learn to play the autoharp can be as interesting to parents as watching a costumed operetta.

There will be occasions when the principal will want to present a group such as the elementary choir. These presentations should grow out of a continuing, on-going program. They should not be imposed superficially in such a way that basic, worthy goals are set aside for spurious, flashy ones.

The principal has frequent opportunities to interpret the instructional program by speaking to civic groups, working in community organizations, conferring with parents, and writing for professional publications. He also interprets the program informally in his day-by-day contacts with members of the community. A principal will talk school whether he is golfing, playing bridge, teaching Sunday School, or chatting with his neighbor over the backyard fence.

The principal who does an effective job of supervising and administering the music program:

1. is himself interested in music.
2. sees the value of music education for girls and boys.
3. recognizes music's unique and important contribution to aesthetic development.
4. recognizes the correlation and enrichment potential of music with other subject areas.
5. indicates a high expectancy for elementary teachers to include music in the daily schedule.
6. insists that the elementary teacher remain in her room during the visit of the consultant.
7. understands the reasons why some teachers are resistant to teaching music.
8. supervises the music program through direct observation.
9. supervises the work of the music specialist.
10. helps define the working role of the music specialist.
11. supervises the work of the instrumental music teacher.
12. plans cooperatively with the consultant and teachers.
13. evaluates the music program.
14. encourages consultant-teacher conferences.
15. encourages and, if necessary, initiates in-service study groups in music education.
16. supplies teachers with needed equipment and instructional materials.
17. seeks additional resource help from the central office.
18. confers with other principals, general supervisors and administrators in regard to the music program.
19. helps interpret the music program to the community.
20. is sensitive to community expectations of the school music program.

Summary

The principal is both the supervisor of instruction as well as the chief administrator of his school. His role as a supervisor is becoming increasingly important. More than any other person, he is influential in establishing the educational climate in his school.

One important supervisory contribution that he alone can make is to indicate very clearly that he expects every teacher to provide for music activities in the daily schedule. Teachers soon learn how their principal feels about the role of music in elementary education. They adjust accordingly.

The principal supervises in many ways: through classroom observation, by working directly with the specialist, by supervising the instrumental teacher if one is assigned, and by continued efforts to improve the curriculum through in-service education. His supervisory functions also include a continuing evaluation of the program.

As an administrator he helps define the role of the music specialist. Desirably, this role should be one of a helping consultant to teachers rather than a specialist teacher of children. The policy is clarified in professional faculty meetings. For the policy to be successful it must have the concurrence of elementary teachers.

The principal is the person who makes recommendations as to purchases of equipment and instructional materials for his school. The approval of requests for the purchase of music equipment, books, and other materials is his responsibility. As the school administrator he represents his needs to the central office staff. He discusses the music program not only with the music specialist but with other principals, general supervisors and top-level administrators.

The principal helps interpret the program to the community through public performances and demonstrations. However, he does not allow entertainment values to overshadow educational considerations. He interprets the program through his professional activities as well as through his informal day-by-day contacts with patrons. He is sensitive as to the expectations patrons have for the music program in his school.

Questions for Discussion

1. How does the principal set the tone for the educational program in his elementary school?
2. Discuss this statement: "The most positive influence the principal can bring to bear is his expectation that each elementary teacher is responsible to teach music."
3. In what ways does the principal actively supervise the music program?
4. What are some administrative responsibilities that the principal has to the music program?
5. What emphasis should be given to instrumental music (instruction on band and orchestra instruments) in the elementary program? At what grade level should instruction begin? If instruction is offered in the elementary school should it be limited to beginning instrumental classes or should the objective be a reasonably well instrumentated band or orchestra?
6. How may the principal foster improved teacher-consultant relationships?
7. How may the principal be helpful in organizing and implementing in-service study groups?
8. What are the principal's responsibilities to the elementary music consultant?
9. Why is it so important that the elementary principal himself be interested in music?
10. How may the supervisor of music and other central office staff members be of assistance to the principal in discharging his supervisory and administrative duties with regard to the music program? Give a number of examples.

12

Responsibilities of
Supervisors and Administrators

The people most directly involved with the elementary music program are the elementary teacher, the specialist, and the principal. However, general supervisors and central office administrators are highly influential in determining the emphasis that is given to the music program. If the school system has an overall director or supervisor of music he is in an excellent position to effect improvement.

In assessing the influence of supervisors and administrators, the supervisor of music will be considered first, then the general supervisor of instruction, and, finally, the central office administrator.

The Supervisor of Music

When there is no appointed supervisor of music, many of the responsibilities outlined here are performed by a general supervisor of instruction. Unless the general supervisor happens to have a depth of background in and an understanding of music, there are some music responsibilities he will be unable to assume. However, a good many of the duties such as coordinating, purchasing instructional materials, hiring personnel, scheduling and evaluating must be done by some member of the central office staff.

When a school board engages a supervisor of music, they are indicating that they cannot provide the kind of program they desire without his help.

131

As the recognized leader in music education in the system, the supervisor of music has an excellent vantage point since he works in all areas and at all levels. This is a distinctive responsibility and a challenging one.

Although he will most certainly be identified with the elective, performing organizations, the supervisor of music should be a champion of the general music program at the elementary, the junior high, and the senior high school level. Experienced supervisors of music agree that there is no more important phase of the music program than the basic classroom offerings in the elementary school. A good part of the supervisor's time is devoted, and rightfully so, to extending and enriching the elementary program. His responsibilities to elementary music may be clarified by considering (1) his supervisory role as a member of the central office staff, (2) his responsibility in coordinating the work of elementary music specialists, and (3) his administrative responsibility.

Staff responsibilities. The supervisor of music is generally recognized as a member of the central office instructional staff. As a staff member he has a unique leadership role. He must not only perceive the music program *in toto,* but he must also see the program within the matrix of the entire educational endeavor. He must be able to relate the unifying principles of music education to the broad aims of education.

Ideally, the supervisor of music should be a well rounded educator with training, experience and depth in the field of music education. He is an educational supervisor with a special competency in music.

The supervisor of music is in close contact with the superintendent and the director of curriculum. He has frequent opportunities to get their reactions and those of other staff members on the needs, interests, and problems of the music program. He literally hammers out a personal philosophy of music education on the basis of many decisions made in conjunction with other staff members.

At staff meetings and on a more informal person-to-person basis he has an opportunity to seek answers to questions on problems related to his field. Perhaps equally important, his reactions and counsel are often sought on matters that lie outside music education.

The relationship that exists between the supervisor of music and elementary principals is a significant one. The supervisor of music is able to discuss things as a matter of course on a peer status. When close cooperation and good understanding exist between him and principals, real progress may be made in elementary music education.

The supervisor of music makes still another contribution by advising the personnel director on professional appointments. The caliber and proficiency of elementary music specialists have a considerable influence on the program. By assisting the director of personnel in selecting the best-qualified person available for each music vacancy, the supervisor of music renders a valuable service in maintaining and improving the competency of the music staff. Although scheduling, working conditions, and materials of instruction all make their respective impressions in shaping the music program, the ability of the elementary music specialists probably contributes most to its effectiveness or ineffectiveness. When the supervisor of music counsels on appointments, he exerts a positive influence on the quality of music instruction.

Supervision of music specialists. Once elementary music specialists are employed, the supervisor of music has specific supervisory responsibilities in planning, organizing, coordinating, and evaluating with them.

He *plans* with elementary music specialists in establishing basic aims and objectives for the elementary program. He works cooperatively in defining grade level goals. He helps the specialist outline her year's work. He is especially concerned in orienting the new elementary music specialist to her duties and he may well spend a number of days with her at the very beginning of her work to assist her in both long-range and short-range planning. He spends considerable time with the new specialist and the principals of the schools to whom she is assigned.

He helps *organize* the work of elementary music specialists. It is largely on his recommendation, with administrative approval, that elementary music specialists are assigned to specific schools. He has found that the most equitable distribution of specialist responsibility is on the basis of the number of teachers served. However, travel problems, relative program strengths, the personality of the specialist, and other factors must be taken into consideration.

With the principal, the supervisor of music helps the elementary music specialist organize her working schedule and clarify her working role within the school. He may also assist the principal and specialist in initiating in-service work, arranging for inter-visitation, and scheduling such groups as class piano, elementary choir, and beginning instrumental classes.

He *coordinates* the work of elementary music specialists. Although the supervisor of music respects differences in approach among individual specialists, he makes certain that all are working toward common, basic goals. He provides for regular, periodic meetings of elementary specialists working within the system to compare procedures, consider mutual problems, evaluate current practice, and chart steps for further improvement. Unless this is done, the specialist soon comes to feel that she is working alone. It is important for the supervisor of music to remember that some problems involving specialists cannot be solved by specialists alone. Occasionally, it will be necessary to invite principals, general supervisors, administrators, or parents to meetings of the specialist group to assist them in seeking solutions to the problems.

The supervisor of music is usually invited to principals' meetings. At these meetings, he not only has an opportunity to react with them on their problems but he is in a position to represent the needs and requests of music specialists as well as to express his own ideas.

Finally, the supervisor of music has the opportunity of *evaluating* with teachers, principals, and specialists. Specialists, particularly, welcome frequent appraisals of their work. Principals also want reactions from the supervisor of music to the question: "How are we doing in music education?" Teachers look to the supervisor of music as a leader in his field. They expect not only general observations but specific, constructive suggestions as to how they may improve their teaching. No matter how extensive his supervisory and administrative responsibilities may be, it is essential that the supervisor of music continue to be identified as an active participant in the elementary program.

Administrative responsibilities. For the supervisor of music, like most supervisors, it is difficult to separate administrative and supervisory functions. Supervision is considered to be the process that has to do directly with the improvement of instruction. Administration is generally regarded to be those processes that facilitate or make instruction possible. More and more, supervision and administration are coming to be looked upon as correlative, coordinate, and complementary rather than separate functions.

A good part of the supervisor of music's administrative responsibilities are related to instructional materials, instruments, and equipment. The preparation of music requisitions is an administrative function that is often delegated to the supervisor of music. Procedures vary, but common practice calls for the initiation of a request for music materials by the teacher, an approval by the principal, the preparation of the requisition by the supervisor of music, and final authorization for purchase by the purchasing agent or business manager.

When delivery is made, the principal or teacher authenticates receipt of the music material as to quantity and quality. The supervisor of music approves the music invoice and submits it to the accounting department for authorization and payment.

The supervisor of music can be particularly helpful in clarifying technical requirements in purchasing. For example, a request for "soprano recorders with baroque fingering" will have little meaning for the purchasing staff. He recommends appropriate sources if they are not specifically designated by the specialist or the principal. Standard school requisition forms and procedures are used for music purchases.

The writing of bid specifications is an exacting job. Specifications are required by school law when large purchases are made. The supervisor of music provides technical help. Purchasing agents can assist the supervisor of music by giving him general suggestions and clarifying legal requirements. Writing specifications involves something of a paradox: first, to write the bid so specifically that equipment of a certain quality is guaranteed, and, second, to write the bids so generally that a large number of merchants may submit competitive bids. Pianos, musical instruments, record players, tape recorders, and music stands are examples of items that may require the preparation of bid specifications by the supervisor of music.

In cooperation with principals, the supervisor of music sees to it that pianos are tuned, instruments are repaired, and record players are serviced. The supervisor of music maintains a current inventory of all items of music equipment in the school system. He prepares the lists of instruments required for insurance purposes. His advice is also sought in planning for periodic replacements as well as for furnishing music rooms in new buildings.

The supervisor of music makes budgetary recommendations to administrative officers. Budget estimates, recommendations for replacement and overhaul, and suggestions for new physical facilities are examples of the kinds of help he offers in this area.

Beyond his supervisory and administrative responsibility for the school system, the supervisor of music is also regarded as the spokesman for music education in the community. As this spokesman, he has an excellent opportunity to interpret the program to patrons as well as to discover their expectations of the music program. The supervisor of music is the logical liaison person for such activities as children's concerts, performances by visiting music groups in the schools, and appearances of school music groups at community functions.

General Supervisors

With a supervisor of music assigned, the general supervisor is usually not as actively or as directly engaged in the supervision of the music program. It may be the policy of the instructional staff for the general supervisor to be concerned only with those subject areas for which there is no specialist supervisor. Of course, if there is no supervisor of music, the general supervisor must also be responsible for music supervision if there is to be coordination from the central office.

Whether or not the general supervisor is directly responsible for music supervision, he should be interested in the program because of his concern for the total learning situation. It is important that he be as interested in the quality of instruction in music as he is in other instruction. It is hoped that he considers music an integral part of elementary education.

This point has been stated several times already but, again, the *attitude* of the general supervisor toward music strongly influences his appraisal of the role it plays in the elementary school. A general supervisor who regards music as significant and important may, in some instances, be more effective in advancing the program with principals and teachers than the specialist or the supervisor of music. The supervisor of music is automatically a "lobbyist" for his special field no matter how broad his outlook may be or how clearly he sees the relationship of music education and general education. A strong recommendation from the general supervisor that all elementary teachers must include music as a part of their classroom work has greater impact than a similar recommendation from the specialist supervisor.

· The goal of the general supervisor is the improvement of the learning situation. In regard to music, like the specialist supervisor, his primary concern is to promote the improvement of music teaching. Although there are many ways in which the general supervisor works, these are fundamental:

1. To help teachers see the basic aims of education and to see how music relates to these aims.
2. To help teachers understand the needs and problems of children and to see how music contributes in meeting them.
3. To help teachers realize their own creative abilities.
4. To orient new teachers as to specialist help available to them.
5. To support teachers' present efforts in music education and, with the help of specialists, show them how to improve them.
6. To assist the principal in providing necessary equipment and instructional materials.
7. To help teachers evaluate the program.

To accomplish these objectives, the general supervisor indicates an interest in music activities whether he is or is not directly responsible for supervising music. Along with the principal, he recommends that teachers remain in the room during the visits of the consultant and encourages them to work cooperatively with her.

He helps organize in-service groups devoted to the improvement of music teaching. An in-service music group in one school is usually part of a system-wide in-service organization coordinated by the general supervisor. It may be that the elementary music consultant would like to hold a series of meetings for all first-grade teachers in the four schools she serves. In such an undertaking, some central office staff member must act as a coordinator.

In conferences with principals, the general supervisor discusses problems relating to the music program along with other curriculum concerns. He works closely with principals in developing a total program of instruction. The supervisor and principal are sensitive to the needs of teachers in regard to music instruction and, with specialist help, they team up to help meet these needs. The general supervisor observes in the classroom, attends faculty meetings, and confers frequently with teachers, specialists and principals.

The very presence of the general supervisor at an in-service music group meeting lends status and value to the project in the eyes of the teacher. It certainly increases the morale of the consultant. The general supervisor can also be helpful in seeing to it that consideration is given to music at pre-school workshops and professional in-service days.

Educational supervision is a leadership function which uses the cooperative process in such ways that all involved in the learning situation have the maximum opportunity to learn. This includes teachers, children, and the specialist. As one aspect of this leadership service, the elementary general supervisor is concerned about the quality of music teaching in the same way that he is concerned about the quality of all teaching.

Administrators

For purposes of this discussion, administrators as considered here are those top-level members of the central office staff such as the superintendent, the director of curriculum, the personnel director, and the director of finance. These men make many of the ultimate decisions regarding the music program. They decide on such matters as the instructional budget, specialist staff, textbooks, and instructional materials. As administrators, their primary function is to facilitate instruction.

It matters very much how the superintendent and his assistants value music both personally and professionally. For example, if the superintendent indicates that music is little more than "frosting on the cake" as far as he is concerned, it is not too surprising if his assistants reflect similar opinions. However, if the superintendent and his staff are genuinely concerned about the unique contributions that music can make to personality fulfillment, this attitude will be apparent in the thoughts and actions of others in the school system. Administrative understanding and cooperation is absolutely essential for the development and maintenance of a well-rounded music program.

The superintendent, as the chief educational administrator for the school board, has the full responsibility for the supervisory program and for the operation of the schools. It is important to bear in mind that administrators, general and special supervisors, and principals serve with delegated responsibilities to assist the superintendent in discharging his overall responsibility to the board and to the people. In other words, the superintendent is the top-level supervisor of the music program as he is of all other programs.

Administrative duties, though widely varied, may be grouped in categories of planning, organizing, coordinating, evaluating, and interpreting. Let us consider how they apply to elementary music education.

Planning. Planning for the elementary music program includes such fundamental questions as *what* is to be taught, *how* it is to be taught, and *who* is to teach it. The way in which administrative officers answer these basic questions determines the emphasis given to the music program. Fortunately, the question, *"Should* music be taught in the elementary school?" has already been answered affirmatively.

Organizing. Organizing the elementary music program depends largely on whether music is taught entirely by specialists, entirely by elementary teachers, or with a cooperative approach involving both. The cooperative approach is the most common pattern although the other two possibilities are found in current practice.

The plan selected will determine the number of specialists to be employed. The number of schools that each will serve, the working role of the specialist, the responsibilities of teachers to music instruction—all of these, in final analysis, are central-office curriculum policy decisions.

Conditions for teaching music that are established at the time of employing elementary teachers are of great importance. If applicants for elementary teaching positions understand *prior* to their employment that they are expected to teach music, they are much more likely to accept this duty in a positive way. In the Central City Schools, the application form for an elementary teaching position includes this question: "Are you qualified to teach music?" The personnel director regards the applicant's affirmative response as a professional commitment.

Both the elementary music specialists and the supervisor of music assist administrative officers in estimating the cost of projected programs. They also recommend to principals the allocation of certain expenditures for music materials and supplies. If the principals and administrative officers view the music program as an integral part of instruction, adequate budgetary provisions will be made for music needs.

Coordinating. Most of the coordination is provided by the supervisor of music. There is a need for articulation between the elementary school, the junior high school, and the senior high school. Consistent goals must be established for music specialists. There must be a clear understanding concerning how each specialist is to work. Specific responsibilities of teachers and principals should be defined through mutual agreement.

Without coordination, the program will be ineffective. Good practices and procedures will not be disseminated. It is perfectly possible that a way of working in one school may be contradictory to an approach used in another school. Although mechanical standardization is not the goal, it is essential that efforts are coordinated so that the movement toward established goals is in the same direction.

However, it is neither expected nor even desirable for curriculum development to proceed at the same pace in all schools. Bona fide curriculum improvement moves forward on a "broken front" basis. It is both unreasonable and unrealistic to expect the program to develop on a uniform front in all classrooms.

Evaluating. Administrative evaluation may be either formal or informal. James Hughes, Supervisor of Music, is evaluating when he responds to the superintendent's question, "Well, Mr. Hughes, how is our music program coming along?" In addition to informal, running evaluations, Mr. Hughes prepares an annual written report that not only summarizes past accomplishments and present status but suggests next steps for continued growth.

The purchasing agent will be interested in knowing from Mr. Hughes how instruments and equipment have performed under actual teaching conditions. The director of instruction asks his opinion as to how a proposed curriculum change may affect music education. A principal in one school will want to know what other faculties think of a particular music series he is considering. The supervisor of music and other administrators, by the very nature of their jobs, are involved in a continuing process of weighing, judging, and evaluating.

From time to time, the administration will schedule formal evaluations of schools for accreditation purposes. Although evaluations of this kind are usually made by a visiting committee, their findings are made available to central office personnel. They provide excellent evaluative instruments for curriculum improvement.

Occasionally, the entire school system in all of its instructional, supervisory, and administrative phases will be painstakingly and thoroughly evaluated by an expert evaluation team. Such an intensive study gives administrative officers, the school board, and the community a complete overview as to the quality of the program of instruction in all areas.

Interpreting. In interpreting the program of instruction to the public, the superintendent is the chief spokesman for the schools. A superintendent who is concerned with the total program will keep the public informed as to developments in the arts as he does in other subject areas. The superintendent is particularly concerned with keeping the school board cognizant of instructional status. In doing so, he may call on the supervisor of music and elementary music specialists to assist him.

Administrative officers can be helpful in establishing guide lines for the entire music staff in regard to public performance. Without a doubt, performances by school music groups have been and will continue to be one of the most effective ways of interpreting the music program. However, particularly at the elementary level, the line between interpretation and exploitation is a fine one. As a rule-of-thumb, administrators should seek an affirmative answer to this question before approving public performances at the elementary level: "Are the interests and learnings of the boys and girls involved of primary concern in scheduling this performance?"

All school people must be sensitive to the needs, interests, and demands of the community. Interpretation is a two-way process: we interpret our program to the public, but, in turn, we must be receptive to suggestions as to the kinds of programs patrons expect to find in their schools.

In this regard, both the music staff and other school people need to remind themselves that one of the primary reasons why we have music in the public schools at all is because parents have indicated in no uncertain terms that they expect the school to provide aesthetic learnings and experiences for their children. No parent wants to slight offerings in language arts, number skills, social studies, or physical education. But they feel very strongly that a "good school" provides experiences in the expressive arts as well.

Summary

General supervisors and administrators are highly influential in determining the emphasis given to the music program. If a supervisor of music is included in the central office staff he can, of course, do much to improve instruction in music. He has the unique advantage of working in all areas of music education. He has the opportunity to react with general supervisors and principals on a peer basis. Perhaps more than any other music educator in the system, he is in a position to see the relationship between music teaching and the total instructional program.

He advises the personnel director on professional appointments. He plans and coordinates the work of elementary music specialists. Administrative responsibilities delegated to him include the task of requisitioning instruments, equipment, and instructional materials. He prepares bid specifications. Along with principals, he is concerned with tuning pianos, repairing instruments, and maintaining music equipment. He is the acknowledged spokesman for music education in the community.

In some instances, the interested general supervisor may advance the cause of music education more effectively than music educators. His recommendations for increased emphasis on music teaching will make a greater impact on principals and elementary teachers than the same recommendations made by the specialist supervisor. The general supervisor's primary reason for being is to bring about instructional improvement, including the improvement of instruction in music.

Administrators make many of the final decisions regarding music education. The attitude of general supervisors and central office administrators to music is important. Administrative understanding and cooperation are essential for the development of a well-rounded music program.

The superintendent has full responsibility to the school board for the instructional program. In this sense, he is the top-level supervisor of music as he is the supervisor of other educational programs. Principals, the supervisor of music, and elementary music specialists are employed to assist the superintendent in discharging his supervisory responsibilities to the board and to the people.

Administrators are responsible for planning, organization, coordination, evaluation, and interpretation. Interpretation must be considered as a two-way process: telling the story to the people as well as listening to their requests and expectations. It is important to remember that one reason why we have music in the public schools is that parents have indicated very clearly that they expect aesthetic experiences for their boys and girls to be included in the elementary curriculum.

Questions for Discussion

1. Are administrative and supervisory responsibilities separate and distinct functions?
2. The supervisor of music is usually on a peer relationship with principals. What implications does this have for the way in which he is able to supervise the elementary music program? How may he be of assistance to the elementary music specialist?

3. Discuss this statement: "The supervisor of music should be an educational supervisor who has a special competency in music."

4. What are the unique supervisory advantages the supervisor of music has as a member of the central office staff?

5. Outline the administrative procedure followed by the supervisor of music in purchasing musical instruments.

6. Why may positive recommendations from the general supervisor to the principal have a greater impact than similar recommendations from the supervisor of music?

7. What are some of the specific things a general supervisor may do to further the aims of elementary music education?

8. In addition to the supervisor of music, what other members of the central office staff are directly concerned in supervising and administering the music program? How does the supervisor of music relate to them in his work?

9. Which professional educator has the ultimate responsibility for the supervision of instruction in a school system?

10. Discuss this statement: "Central office administrators, general and special supervisors serve with delegated responsibilities to assist the superintendent in discharging his responsibility to the board of education."

13

How Is the Program Evaluated?

We evaluate everything in our daily living either consciously or sub-consciously. We select, reject, improve, and refine. Evaluation is a part of every human endeavor. Without evaluation, it is impossible to tell whether or not we are moving toward our objectives. In education, evaluation is a method of making valid judgments concerning ways of improving instruction. It is a process whereby we make observations, collect data, draw conclusions, and revise procedures.

Certainly there is as great a need for continuing evaluation in music education as in any other undertaking. The process of evaluation is an important one for the elementary music specialist and for all others concerned with the elementary music program.

General Criteria

1. Evaluating is a *continuing* process. Although it is desirable to engage in a formal evaluation periodically, it is important to bear in mind that a running appraisal of one's day-by-day work is highly significant. Formal or informal evaluations point to next steps which, once placed into action, call for still further appraisals.

2. Evaluation, unlike measurement, is not a precise, objective process.

The very nature of teaching and the multiplicity of relationships involved make the development of a scientific, infallible set of criteria impossible. However, even with the realization that the evaluation of music teaching is in many ways subjective, it is an essential process that gives us valuable information concerning current practice and suggests guidelines for further curriculum development.

3. Evaluation includes a number of well-defined steps. Whether the evaluation is on an individual basis or a team approach, the procedure involves:

a. Setting up goals and criteria.
b. Examining current practice and gathering facts.
c. Determining to what extent practices observed compare with the evaluative criteria and the established goals.
d. Charting next steps for instructional improvement.

4. The purpose of evaluation is to help us decide how well we are achieving the primary aim of supervision: the improvement of instruction. Improvement implies change in children, in teaching methods, in the learning climate. We need to find out how well we are succeeding in bringing about desired changes. We are interested in strengths and weaknesses. We are particularly interested in identifying those problems on which we can bring about change with the staff, budget, and facilities at our disposal.

In music education, we are concerned to what extent musical learnings are taking place in the classroom. The paramount criterion for evaluating the effectiveness of a program of music education is its effect on the musical behavior of students themselves.

Appraisals, to a degree, are subjective. They are made in terms of values held by the appraiser. Some quantitative evaluations may be made: We can make an inventory of the number of textbooks, record players, recordings, and instruments. However, when we begin to examine such items as the following, completely objective criteria are not applicable:

1. Increased musical responsiveness of students.
2. Increased musical knowledge and understanding for teachers and students.
3. Increased skills on the part of the elementary teacher in teaching music.
4. Enriched musical opportunities in the classroom.
5. Increased skill on the part of students in performing music.
6. Deepened appreciation of music on the part of students and teachers.

All of these objectives call for value judgments. It is not only conceivable but also possible that three different evaluators may make three different appraisals of the same learning situation. The key criterion should be the increased musicality of students.

There are a number of standardized, published tests dealing with musical aptitude and musical achievement that are applicable to the elementary music program. They include:

Musical aptitude

Drake Musical Aptitude Test
Printed tests: Public School Publishing Co., Bloomington, Illinois, 1934.
Recordings: Kent State University, Kent, Ohio, 1942.
Age 8 to adult.

Gaston Test of Musicality
Streep Music Company, Inc., 913 Grand Ave., Kansas City, Missouri, 1950.
Grades 4 to 12.

Kwalwasser-Dykema Music Test
Carl Fischer, Inc., 56 Cooper Square, New York, N.Y., 1930.
Grades 4 to 12.

Kwalwasser Music Talent Test
Mills Music Company, 1619 Broadway, New York, N.Y., 1953.
Grades 4 to 12.

Seashore Measures of Musical Talent
Psychological Corporation, 522 Fifth Ave., New York, N.Y., revised 1939.
Grade 5 to adult.

Tilson-Gretsch Musical Aptitude Test
Fred Gretsch Co., 218 South Wabash Ave., Chicago, Illinois, 1941.
Grades 4 to 12.

Musical achievement

Beach Music Test
Bureau of Educational Measurements, Kansas State Teachers College, Emporia, Kansas, revised 1932.
Grade 4 to adult.

Gildersleeve Music Achievement Test
Bureau of Publications, Teachers College, Columbia University, New York, N.Y., 1933.
Grades 4 to 8.

Jones Music Recognition Test
Carl Fischer, Inc., 56 Cooper Square, New York, N.Y., 1949.
Part I: Elementary and junior high school.

Kelsey Standardized Tests of Musical Achievement
C. A. Gregory Company, 345 Calhoun St., Cincinnati, Ohio, 1931.
Grades 3 to 6.

Knuth Achievement Tests in Music
Educational Test Bureau, Inc., 720 Washington Ave., S.E., Minneapolis, Minnesota, 1936.
Grades 7 to 12.

Kotick-Torgerson Diagnostic Tests of Achievement in Music
California Test Bureau, 5916 Hollywood Blvd., Los Angeles, California, 1950.
Grades 4 to 12.

These tests, like standardized tests in any field, should be considered as indicative rather than definitive. They are valuable instruments in conducting an evaluation of the elementary music program. Selected tests should be carefully screened and tested before they are used widely for evaluative purposes.

Staff Self-evaluation

All who are involved in the teaching-learning situation should have a part in establishing evaluative criteria. Those who are directly concerned include the teacher, the consultant, the principal, the supervisor of music, general supervisors, and administrators.

The elementary music consultant, perhaps more than any other person involved in the elementary music program, is engaged in continuous evaluation. A daily appraisal of her work is both practical and necessary.

The consultant is particularly concerned about the effectiveness of her own contributions. It is important that she take the time to weigh the effects of a particular way of working and to assess, as fairly as possible, the extent to which it contributes to improved practice.

It is important to bear in mind that the personal qualities and attitudes of the elementary music consultant are at least as important as her technical qualifications. If the consultant is tactless, acts superior, and remains aloof, the teachers will not seek her help no matter how musically competent she may be.

On the following pages are outlines of several sets of criteria. The statements are so formulated that one may react by using these evaluative checks:

E   The provision or condition is met *extensively.*
M   The provision or condition is met to a *moderate* degree.
N   The provision or condition is not met but *needed.*
Q   The provision or condition is not met but its need is *questioned.*
O   The provision or condition is not met but it is not considered desirable for this situation.

To illustrate, if the statement concerning the self-analysis of the consultant which reads: "Understands the developmental characteristics of elementary children" is answered with an *M,* the consultant is indicating that she does understand developmental characteristics to a moderate degree.

Consultant self-appraisal

    ————— possesses the necessary personal traits for working with people: impartiality, courteousness, patience, ability to take criticism, ability to put self in the other person's position.

_____ has a broad, general education.

_____ has had extensive training in the field of elementary music education.

_____ has had applied music work in voice and piano and is a creditable performer.

_____ has had professional training in elementary education.

_____ is certified in elementary music education.

_____ has a broad outlook, is able to relate the objectives of music education to general education.

_____ understands the developmental characteristics of children.

_____ works creatively.

_____ has high standards for herself, has a positive attitude towards her role in elementary education.

_____ works democratically, thinks in terms of "our" program rather than "my" program.

_____ has a clear idea as to specific grade level aims, goals, and learnings.

_____ has a personal philosophy of music education expressed in writing.

_____ participates in action research, is informed on pertinent research findings.

_____ continues to add to her professional library of books, music, pamphlets, and recordings.

_____ helps interpret the elementary music program to the community.

_____ participates in community activities.

Consultant's ability to work with individual teachers

_____ has faith in the ability of elementary teachers to teach music.

_____ makes effective classroom visits, is welcomed by teachers and students.

_____ her working role is clearly established and is well understood by teachers and principals.

_____ helps teachers feel secure, relieves anxiety of the "musically timid" teacher.

_____ is successful in building a positive attitude toward music on the part of teachers.

_____ develops the musicality of teachers.

_____ knows each teacher well, is on a first name basis with most of them.

_____ discovers and utilizes special talents of teachers.

_____ relates consistently with teachers on a person-to-person basis.

_____ provides a diversity of stimuli for teachers.

_____ encourages experimentation on the part of teachers.

_____ is able to help individual teachers define their problems.

_____ receives frequent "on call" requests from teachers.

_____ is tactful, does not disrupt the classroom routine.

_____ attempts to answer each request for help, does not make any promises she cannot keep.

_____ shares recognition and praise for the program with teachers.

_____ commends teachers for their achievements.

_____ gives special attention to new, inexperienced teachers.

_____ confers frequently with teachers.

Consultant's ability in group processes

_____ understands the nature of the group process.

_____ organizes and conducts in-service groups in music education.

_____ participates as a member of an in-service group on general educational problems.

_____ is invited to participate in faculty meetings.

_____ functions democratically as a group member or leader.

_____ conducts music education workshops.

_____ meets regularly with other music consultants in the system.

_____ meets with the total music staff.

_____ participates actively in professional meetings on district, regional, and state levels.

_____ is a member of district, regional, state, and national professional organizations.

_____ acts as a liaison person for the school with community music groups.

Consultant's skill in administration

_____ keeps principals and administrators informed about status of the program.

_____ provides for an exchange of ideas and practices through mimeographed memoranda and bulletins.

_____ plans her supervisory schedule with principals and teachers.

_____ informs principals and administrators of budgetary needs.

_____ recommends appropriate materials of instruction.

_____ assists the principal in evaluating materials.

_____ assists the principal in requisitioning materials.

_____ promotes effective utilization of materials.

_____ assists the principal in providing for maintenance of equipment: tuning pianos, servicing record players, repairing and replacing instruments.

_____ assists the principal in keeping an inventory of music equipment.

_____ when invited to do so, assists the supervisor of music and administrators in preparing bid specifications.

In addition to the elementary music specialist, the elementary teacher and the principal are directly involved in the elementary music program. The following self-evaluation checklist is suggested for the teacher in the classroom.

The elementary teacher

_____ accepts her responsibility for music teaching.

_____ has a positive attitude toward music, is enthusiastic about teaching music.

_____ is prepared to teach music.

_____ recognizes the contribution music makes to the growth and development of children.

_____ teaches music daily.

_____ remains in the classroom and actively participates during the consultant's visit.

_____ advises the consultant of her needs.

_____ makes specific requests for help to the consultant.

_____ is aware of accepted activities and approaches in music for her grade level.

_____ takes part in in-service music activities.

_____ is familiar with the available materials of instruction in music.

_____ has and makes use of the teacher's manual for the elementary music series.

_____ uses recordings and other audio-visual aids.

_____ takes into consideration individual differences in teaching music.

_____ shares successful techniques and procedures in music teaching with other teachers.

_____ evaluates her own music teaching continuously.

_____ keeps parents informed of their child's progress in music.

The principal is also involved in the evaluation process. The following self-evaluation checklist is suggested for him.

The elementary principal

_____ indicates a high degree of expectancy concerning the responsibility of elementary teachers to teach music.

_____ is himself interested and enthusiastic about music in the elementary school.

_____ recognizes music for its aesthetic contribution.

_____ actively supervises the classroom music program.

_____ supervises the work of the elementary music consultant.

_____ confers frequently with the consultant and teachers about the music program.

_____ provides adequate time for music in the daily schedule.

_____ with the assistance of teachers, prepares the visiting schedule of the consultant so that she may be of optimum service.

_____ encourages consultant-teacher conferences.

_____ supervises the work of the instrumental music teacher if one is assigned.

_____ arranges for inter-visitation.

_____ promotes and initiates in-service training.

_____ relays "on call" requests from the teachers to the consultant.

_____ makes music books available to each child.

_____ provides an adequate record player for every classroom.

_____ provides other necessary materials of instruction and equipment such as autoharps, rhythm band instruments, and recordings.

_____ provides books for reference purposes and general reading on music in the school library.

_____ provides special music for choirs and instrumental groups.

_____ confers with other principals and administrative officials concerning the music program in his school.

_____ evaluates the music program.

_____ helps interpret the program to parents and patrons.

Group Evaluation

Thus far we have considered the self-evaluation of the elementary music consultant, the teacher, and the principal. They also participate with other professional workers in *group* evaluation.

There will be many times when appraisals must involve the entire faculty. It is quite possible that some evaluations will apply to more than one school. In a system-wide evaluation, for example, principals from several schools and teachers in many subject areas are invited to participate. On broad questions of policy, school board members and patrons of the community evaluate with professional educators.

In a group evaluation, each individual is given the opportunity to make his individual appraisal and to express his personal opinions. However, it is essential that he be open-minded and broad-minded enough to analyze and interpret findings with the group. Such a group evaluation can be very helpful to the individual by enabling him to see more clearly the relation of his area to the total instructional program.

Some examples of group or team evaluation are:

1. Working cooperatively with the local faculty in evaluating the music program of the school.
2. Serving with fellow teachers, principals, and administrators in a system-wide evaluation.
3. Cooperating with other members of the music staff in an overall evaluation of the total music program.
4. Working with a group of parents and professional workers in an evaluation of school-community relations.
5. Serving as a member of a visiting committee to evaluate a program in another school system.

Program Evaluation

In an evaluation of the music program, it is necessary to reemphasize that the process is not limited to specialists in music education. All who are directly or indirectly involved with elementary music education should have an opportunity to establish the criteria. In addition to music specialists, the teachers, principals, general supervisors, and administrators should evaluate the music program. From time to time, it will be desirable to include parents and patrons in the process.

The evaluator brings to the task a number of assumptions. In keeping with our point of view these basic assumptions are made:

1. Music is considered primarily as a significant learning in its own right and secondarily as an enrichment subject.
2. The music program begins with the developing personality.
3. The musical growth of children may be fostered only through rich, vital, and varied musical experiences.
4. The program must be geared as closely as possible to the developmental characteristics of children.
5. The program must be sufficiently broad so that all students may take effective, participating roles.

For evaluation purposes, we may consider the music program in five large categories: (1) focus, (2) scope, (3) instruction, (4) organization, and (5) resources. Let us consider each of these categories.

1. *Focus.* What is the focus of the program? In simple terms, the focus of the program should be on the musical responsiveness of the developing personality.

This may appear so obvious as to be unnecessary to state it at all. However, it is so fundamental that its acceptance or rejection will set the pattern for the entire music program, or for any program of education.

An emphasis on human values is a philosophy difficult to evaluate statistically. Yet when teachers are firmly committed to this philosophy, it is manifested in so many ways that there can be no doubt as to its presence as a guiding principle.

The philosophy or point of view should be expressed in written form. A statement in and of itself will not guarantee the desired program. However, the lack of a carefully formulated statement suggests that there has been little serious attention on the part of the music staff to establish a common point of view. The act of writing such a statement demands cooperative staff effort.

Not only should a statement of the basic philosophy be in writing, but broad objectives should be outlined consistent with the point of view taken.

These objectives need not be overly detailed. They should serve as guide lines to those responsible for the day-by-day realization of the program.

The following criteria are helpful in evaluating program focus:

_____ the major aim of the program is the development of musical responsiveness.

_____ a written statement setting forth the staff's philosophy of music education has been prepared.

_____ the long-range objectives are clearly established.

_____ these objectives are consistent with the philosophy of the school and school system.

_____ the program is organized and operated so as to achieve these objectives.

_____ there is evidence of progress toward long-range goals.

_____ a curriculum guide for elementary music has been prepared by the local staff.

_____ the music program is an integral part of the school.

_____ the music program is closely related to the child's world.

_____ the objectives of the music program are known to all elementary teachers.

_____ the aims and objectives are reevaluated periodically and, if necessary, revised.

_____ the objectives of the music program have the support and approval of the administration.

_____ the objectives of the music program have the support and approval of the community.

2. *Scope.* The program should be of sufficient scope so that a rich, highly varied program is provided to meet the needs of all children. Music offerings should be considered in the light of the contribution they make to diverse emotional satisfactions and intellectual understandings of boys and girls.

The music activities include not only singing but listening, moving, playing, creating, and reading. In addition to classroom experiences, other activities such as elementary choir, class piano, beginning orchestra, and beginning band are inevitable developments of a virile program. Assembly singing is an important aspect of the total program.

The following criteria are helpful in evaluating the scope of the program:

_____ the music program provides for aesthetic, emotional, and intellectual development.

_____ singing is given adequate consideration.

_____ listening to music is given adequate consideration.

_____ moving in physical response to music is given adequate consideration.

_____ playing classroom instruments is given adequate consideration.

_____ creative activities are given adequate consideration.

_____ reading notation is given adequate consideration.

_____ the program provides for individual differences.

_____ the classroom program is regarded as the basic offering.

_____ provision is made for assembly singing, with some singing included in every school assembly.

_____ elementary choir is available to interested students.

_____ beginning string classes are available.

_____ beginning wind classes are available.

_____ beginning brass classes are available.

_____ beginning percussion classes are available.

_____ class piano is available.

_____ the music program is a vital influence in the life of the school.

_____ the program reflects interests and needs of the community.

_____ the program draws on musical resources of the community.

3. *Instruction.* How effective is the instruction? The answer lies in determining how well the philosophy and objectives developed by the staff are carried out in actual practice. An appraisal involves an evaluation of the kinds of musical experiences provided for children in the elementary school.

Instructional practices should indicate that music is regarded as a unique and significant learning by teachers, principals, and specialists. The instruction should be centered on musical learnings to a far greater degree than on extra-musical learnings. Growth in musicality should be the central theme.

Instruction must coincide with the developmental readiness of children. It should be characterized by imagination and spontaneity. The appropriateness of the experiences provided can best be determined by critically observing the attitude, response, and awareness of the student himself.

Attitude is difficult to evaluate. Colwell has the following direct suggestion for determining student attitude toward music that the writer has found to be remarkably effective. Although his comments are made in terms of the secondary level, the same procedure may be adapted by the elementary teacher.

> A simple device which is a valid method for discovering pupil attitude is to have the pupil rank his school subjects in order of preference, this to be done in homeroom or some other impartial atmosphere. Such a ranking is both simpler and more accurate than any published test known to the author.[1]

This type of student evaluation is very easy to administer and it is quite revealing. For obvious reasons, it should be given by the elementary teacher when the consultant is not present.

[1] Richard Colwell, "Evaluation: Its Use and Significance," Music Educators Journal, February–March, 1963, p. 49.

The following criteria are helpful in evaluating instruction:

_____ children respond positively to music instruction.

_____ children are growing in musical taste and discrimination.

_____ learning experiences are organized with a regard for the developmental characteristics and abilities of children.

_____ activities are sequentially planned in terms of the development of musical skills.

_____ attention is given to responding to the mood of music.

_____ attention is given to the study of the relation of the text to the music.

_____ attention is given to the study of melody.

_____ attention is given to the study of rhythm.

_____ attention is given to the study of form.

_____ attention is given to the study of harmony.

_____ music instruction is offered daily.

_____ there is evidence of careful planning and preparation for music teaching.

_____ music is correlated with other curriculum areas.

_____ in-service opportunities are provided for elementary teachers.

_____ in-service opportunities are provided for elementary music specialists.

_____ general supervisors observe and appraise the program.

_____ opportunities are available for public performance.

4. *Organization.* Is the program organized efficiently? We are concerned here with the organization of learning experiences, the specialist's schedule, articulation between the elementary and secondary school, and overall coordination and administrative support.

The following criteria are helpful in evaluating program organization:

_____ there is organizational continuity in the program from grade to grade.

_____ clear-cut goals are established for each grade level.

_____ there is articulation between the program of the elementary school and the secondary school.

_____ there is a supervisor of music responsible for the overall music program.

_____ consultant service on a weekly basis is provided by the elementary music consultant to each teacher.

_____ the working role of the specialist is well defined and is understood by all concerned.

_____ there is administrative expectancy for the elementary teacher to teach music.

_____ the music staff is well organized.

_____ the elementary music specialist is considered a member of the school faculty.

_____ channels of communication are well established and always open between the consultant and teachers, principals, and administrators.

_____ a prescribed procedure is established and followed for securing instructional materials.

_____ schedules for special music groups such as the elementary choir and beginning instrumental classes are planned cooperatively by the music teacher, classroom teachers, principals, and instructional supervisors.

5. *Resources.* Resources include instructional materials such as textbooks, teachers' manuals, supplementary music series, and special music. Resources also include pianos, record players, recordings, classroom instruments and standard instruments. Books on music for reference and for general reading should be available in the school library or in individual classrooms. In regard to physical facilities, it is unusual for a special music room to be provided unless the music teacher does all of the teaching of music. However, assigned space is necessary for such activities as elementary choir, beginning instrumental classes, and class piano.

The following criteria are helpful in evaluating resources and materials:

_____ adequate financial support is given to the elementary music program.

_____ a music textbook is available to every student.

_____ a teacher's manual is provided for every teacher.

_____ the selected music series provides music of high quality and appeal.

_____ supplementary song books are available to the teachers and students.

_____ a good quality record player is standard classroom equipment.

_____ record players are maintained in good working order.

_____ correlated recordings for the basal series are available.

_____ at least one of the basic record libraries for the elementary school is available for listening experiences.

_____ each school has a number of such classroom instruments as autoharps, resonator bells, xylophones, and rhythm instruments.

_____ reference and general reading books on music are available.

_____ at least one good piano is provided for each school, with more desirable.

_____ pianos are tuned at least twice a year.

_____ a tape recorder is available in each school.

_____ visual aids such as charts, pictures of instruments, flannel boards, and film strips are available.

_____ special provision is made in the school budget for providing materials of instruction for the music specialist.

_____ there is a long-range plan for the systematic replacement of pianos, record players, and instruments.

_____ special music is available for the instrumental classes, elementary chorus, and piano classes.

_____ assigned space is provided for the special music classes.

_____ films on music are available from local or state film libraries.

_____ risers are available for the elementary chorus.

There is of course no recommended "grade" on this evaluative check list. Its purpose is to appraise the program in a comprehensive way, to point up strengths and weaknesses, and to suggest next steps for continued improvement.

A great many *E's* (the provision or condition is met extensively) would indicate that the appraiser is of the opinion that the program is very effective. A great many *M's* (the provision or condition is met to a moderate degree) would indicate that the appraiser feels that the program is adequate in many areas. A great many *N's* (the provision is not met but needed) would point up particular areas where special attention is needed. This category suggests a good many "next steps" that might be taken in improvement. *Q's* on the checklist (the provision or condition is not met but its need is questioned) suggest the possibility for staff discussion. *O's* (the provision or condition is not met but is not desirable) indicate a rejection of a particular criterion on the part of the evaluator.

A good way to summarize the overall evaluation is to ask these four questions:

1. What are the outstanding strong points of our elementary music program?
2. What are the obvious weaknesses of our program?
3. What immediate steps may be taken to improve the program?
4. What long-range plans must be made to.achieve aims and objectives?

Summary

Music education, like any other educational endeavor, must be continuously evaluated. The evaluation process is important not only for the music specialist, but for everyone who is directly or indirectly involved with the elementary music program. The evaluation process includes setting up criteria, observing and gathering facts, appraising practices, and charting next steps. Although certain aspects of the elementary music program may be evaluated objectively, a good many of the evaluative criteria call for value judgments. The ultimate goal of evaluation is the improvement of instruction.

The consultant evaluates her own contributions to the program. She is concerned not only with a personal self-appraisal but with her ability to work with individual teachers, her ability in group processes, and her administrative ability. Checklists were also suggested for the elementary teacher and the elementary principal.

In evaluating the program itself, the evaluative criteria were grouped in five major categories: focus, scope, instruction, organization, and resources. The categories are not mutually exclusive. They offer a broad, comprehensive look at the overall elementary music program.

In summarizing the detailed evaluations, it is suggested that these four questons be considered: (1) What are the strong points? (2) What are the weak points? (3) What immediate steps should be taken? (4) What long range plans should be made?

Questions for Discussion

1. Why is evaluation an essential part of every human endeavor? Give several examples outside the field of education.
2. What is the distinction between formal and informal evaluation?
3. Outline the steps of the evaluative process.
4. What are some things in music education which may be evaluated objectively? Some which call for subjective judgments?
5. Investigate one of the published tests listed in this chapter. Report your findings to the class.
6. Why is it important that the philosophy or point of view of the staff be expressed in writing? Assume that you are the supervisor of music of a staff that includes twenty music teachers. How would you go about preparing such a statement?
7. Under what circumstances might the elementary music consultant be involved in group evaluation?
8. Discuss this statement: "The appraiser brings to the task of evaluation a set of values and assumptions."
9. What are some of the considerations involved in evaluating the scope of the program?
10. What are some of the considerations involved in evaluating the quality of instruction?

Part Four

Elementary Music
Supervision in Perspective

14

How Did Elementary
Music Supervision Evolve?

It is surprising that many educators, including music educators, look on teaching music in schools as a comparatively recent development. Actually, the teaching of music in school goes back to the days of our earliest civilizations. By reviewing the significant developments in music education we may better understand the role of the elementary music specialist in today's schools. An attempt to understand the principles of elementary music supervision must give consideration to the history of music education as well as to the development of instructional supervision.

Our Heritage in Music Education

Ancient Greece (fourth century B.C. to second century A.D.). No other civilization has contributed more to the well-being of modern man than that developed on the peninsula of Greece. A handful of men produced the philosophy, the art, and the drama which influence us even today. The Greeks taught us the meaning of beauty, the artistry of form and design, the strength of logic, and the value of truth.

The end sought by the *polis* or city-state was the good life. Art and music were integrally bound up in the civic, religious, and social life of Athens in a way seldom approached in later history. However, the word *music* did not have the same meaning then that it holds for us. As the Greeks conceived it, music was everything that trained the soul in contradistinction to gymnastics which trained the body. Music meant not only performing, listening to, and discussing music but it also included such areas of learning as letters, dancing, art, and dramatics.

Butts describes the curriculum in this manner:

> By the third century B.C. the liberal arts of Greece were more or less commonly regarded as including on the elementary level, grammar, gymnastics, music, and sometimes drawing and on the advanced level, arithmetic, geometry, astronomy, musical harmony, logic, rhetoric, and philosophy.[1]

Music was given a preferred status largely because of its intellectual value. Pythagoras discovered mathematical consistencies in tonal relationships. Plato was among the first to emphasize the extrinsic values of music, primarily on the basis of Pythagoras' findings. For many educators, the justification of music is still made on extrinsic rather than intrinsic values.

Ancient Rome (eighth century B.C. to sixth century A.D.). In Rome, music became even more of an intellectual undertaking than it had been in Greece. In Cicero's day, music was recognized as one of the seven liberal arts. These arts were regarded as those studies necessary to the development of the cultivated man. They were the arts that "liberated" the human spirit. At a basic level the arts included the *trivium* (grammar, rhetoric, and logic), and at a more advanced level the *quadrivium* (arithmetic, geometry, astronomy, and music). The sequence is given in an ascending order of importance with music in the preferred place. However, as in Greece, music meant the broad area of the fine arts.

The Middle Ages (sixth century to the thirteenth century A.D.). In the Middle Ages the seven liberal arts continued to dominate the curriculum. Music was studied as an intellectual discipline rather than as a performing art. A formidable body of music theory was developed. Music was considered as a prerequisite to the study of medicine, law, religion, and other advanced work.

The cathedral schools of the Middle Ages in their dualistic preoccupation with mind and matter gave more than passing attention to the study of music. In fact, the training of musicians in such schools as the *scholae cantorum* was one of the major activities in early Christian education.

In addition to the cathedral schools, parish churches in small villages provided elementary instruction in reading, writing, and music. The emphasis was on reading Latin and taking part in church services. In the palaces, the typical training for the young squire included not only reading, writing,

---

[1] R. Freeman Butts, *A Cultural History of Education* (New York: McGraw-Hill Book Company, 1947), p. 103.

and the courtly graces but he was also taught how to sing and to play a musical instrument.

There was little opportunity for the common man to study music at the cathedral school or the palace school. Among the peasants, musical traditions were handed down from father to son. This is the period that saw the emergence of *troubadours* and *trouvères*. Eventually *meistersingers* appeared on the scene as fully recognized guild craftsmen.

The Renaissance (fourteenth to the sixteenth centuries). The ideal man of the Renaissance was a broadly educated person capable of assuming leadership in both the church and the state. Under the philosophy of Humanism, the development of the individual was of prime importance. The seven medieval liberal arts, including music, were the guidelines for "gentlemanly" education.

One important change occurred in music. Renaissance music was not regarded primarily as an intellectual, theoretical study. It was prized for its beauty, for its uniqueness, and for its expressiveness. Music instruction was standard practice in schools sponsored by the court and the church. The training of apprentices in the music guilds had even more far-reaching effects.

The Reformation (sixteenth and seventeenth centuries). Perhaps the outstanding characteristic of the Reformation was the establishment of vernacular schools, schools that used the native tongue of the area. Boys and girls were instructed in reading, writing, arithmetic, music, and religion.

The growing use of printed books and Luther's translation of the Bible into German accelerated the use of the vernacular. The Bible, the catechism, and Luther's hymnal were used in addition to other textbooks. Similar materials, with appropriate adaptations, were used in the vernacular schools of the Calvinists and Catholics.

The Reformation had a profound influence on school music instruction. Luther himself was a skilled musician and composer. Music, particularly singing, was emphasized in the elementary curriculum.

Developments in North America

Earliest evidences. Britton cites evidence that the first school in North America was not in the New England colonies, but in Mexico.[2] Pedro de Gante, a lay-brother of the Franciscan order, founded a school in the ancient city of Tezcoco as early as 1524. Founded on the model of the European cathedral school, it included the teaching of music in the curriculum.

To the Spanish Britton also ascribes the distinction of instituting music instruction in what was to become the United States. In 1540 in the area we

[2] Allen P. Britton, "Music in Early American Public Education: A Historical Critique," in *Basic Concepts in Music Education,* ed. Nelson B. Henry (Chicago: National Society for the Study of Education, Fifty-Seventh Yearbook, 1958), p. 197.

now know as New Mexico, a priest established a mission school that included music.[3] Instruction in music in the mission schools of the far West continued for many years.

We know that early Catholic missionaries, both priests and laymen, brought not only religious instruction but also the traditions of European music to the colonists and Indians in the early settlements of Canada and the eastern seaboard of the United States. The Puritans and Calvinists also brought their music with their religion though it was Protestant psalmody instead of Catholic liturgical music.

Music education in Colonial America. In general, there was not much provision for the arts in colonial New England. There was little attempt to emphasize the role of music as a fine art in the schools. Music in the colonies was primarily for the church.

There were no large cathedrals, no guilds, and no courts to advance the cause of music as in Europe. The primary concern of the colonist was to survive in a hostile land. As Leonhard and House analyze it, "Although these conditions soon abated in the more settled areas, the environmental struggle has been a continuing one in America. Perhaps this is responsible for a certain materialistic, nonartistic climate of opinion that still persists."[4]

It is significant, however, that the *Bay Psalm Book* was one of the first books published in the colonies. Printed in 1640, it was a metrical version of the psalms intended to be sung to well-known tunes. Musical notation was not included until the ninth edition was printed in 1698.[5]

Britton points out that one of the earliest evidences of music education in colonial America occurred in Pennsylvania in 1694 when German settlers, led by John Kelpius, organized schools in which their children were given instruction in music. As Britton puts it, "What is important to remember is that these Americans saw to it that music was taught in the first schools they organized."[6]

The Singing School. The most dramatic development in American music education in the eighteenth century was the singing school. "Such schools (actually, evening classes convened at any convenient hall) are known to have existed as early as 1712, but by 1721 they were flourishing in New England."[7] Taught by a traveling singing master, the classes met for three to four weeks with one or two lessons scheduled each week. In return for a modest fee, the itinerant teacher taught adults and children to sing. The primary objective was to improve congregational singing. The relation-

---

[3] *Ibid.,* p. 197.

[4] Charles Leonhard and Robert W. House, *Foundations and Principles of Music Education* (New York: McGraw-Hill Book Company, 1959), p. 49.

[5] Edward Bailey Birge, *History of Public School Music in the United States* (Philadelphia: Theodore Presser Co., 1937, revised), p. 5.

[6] Britton, "Music in Early American Education," p. 198.

[7] Allen P. Britton, "Music Education: An American Specialty," Music Educators Journal, June–July 1962, p. 27.

ship of music teaching and religious education has been noted in several instances in earlier periods.

Singing masters included such illustrious names as William Billings and Francis Hopkinson. The singing school always remained a private rather than a tax-supported enterprise. It flourished for some 150 years. For music educators, it is important to remember that the singing school was an attempt to bring music to the average person in a simple, practical form and in a manner in which he could participate effectively. These are still primary endeavors in music education today.

The Nineteenth Century

Nineteenth-century education in America was strongly influenced by the work of Johann Heinrich Pestalozzi in Switzerland. Pestalozzi "broadened the conception of what the elementary curriculum should contain, and perhaps more than any other single person, helped to introduce into the elementary curriculum instruction in geography and nature study, drawing, and music along with the more commonly accepted studies of reading, writing, and arithmetic."[8] Pestalozzi was not only a theorist; he actually put his ideas into practice in his school at Yverdon, Switzerland. He saw in music one of the disciplines for developing the perceptive powers of the child. He was interested not only in the child's intellectual potential, but also in his moral and physical development as well.

The ideas of Pestalozzi were brought to America by educators such as E. A. Sheldon, superintendent of schools in Oswego, New York; William Woodbridge, superintendent of schools in Boston; and Horace Mann. Pestalozzi's work became widely known in American education influencing, among others, Lowell Mason. Pestalozzi's principles, as they applied to music, may be summarized as follows:

To teach sounds before symbols.
To learn through observation rather than telling.
To teach one thing at a time.
To learn each step well before going on to the next.
To give theory and principles only after the music has been experienced.

In America, the transition from singing schools to the first school music programs was not a revolutionary transformation since the first school music teachers were also singing school masters. The first public school music classes were, in fact, transplanted singing schools. As the masters were engaged to become school teachers, they gave up their itinerant work. It is not at all surprising that the first textbooks in the schools closely resembled the psalm books of the singing school.

[8] Butts, *A Cultural History*, p. 426.

The most prominent and most influential of the singing school and singing convention directors who became a school teacher was Lowell Mason. He applied the Pestalozzian principles, as he understood them, to the study of music in his singing school handbook, *Manual of Instruction*, published in 1834. Although we recognize the year 1838 as the milestone for the beginning of music education in American schools, it is interesting to note that Mason worked on an experimental basis during the 1837–38 school year at the Hawes Hall School in South Boston without pay. When Mason first presented his plan to board members, it was evident that they were dubious about his proposal, "Whereupon Lowell Mason offered to give his services as teacher of music for a year in one of the schools of the city, and furnish his own books and equipment."[9] The experiment worked well for "on August 28, 1838, a fortnight after the exhibition [of Hawes School children] the school board passed a vote to the effect that the committee on music be instructed to contract with a teacher of vocal music in the several schools of the city of Boston."[10] Lowell Mason, along with four assistants, was employed to inaugurate a program of vocal music *in the elementary schools*. Music was not added to the Boston high school curriculum until 1869.

The great significance of the Boston schoolboard's action in 1838 was not in *allowing* music to be taught. Music had been offered on an informal basis in many schools prior to this time. Although Mason was the most influential pioneer in school music teaching, he was not necessarily the first. The significance of the action of the Boston schoolboard was that school officials recognized the *validity of music as a school subject* along with reading, grammar, and arithmetic. It is also interesting to observe that the development came neither from action taken by the board, nor from the initiative of the central office, nor even from interested patrons. The action was initiated by Lowell Mason.

His influence soon spread across the country. In much the same way as in Boston, other major cities such as Buffalo (1843), Pittsburgh (1844), Cincinnati (1846), and Chicago (1848) placed music in the curriculum of the elementary school.[11] Music was the first of the expressive arts to take its place in the curriculum of the American public schools. Offerings in the fine arts and dramatics soon followed.

Concerning early supervisory practice in music education, Birge has this to say:

> This specialist teacher was not a supervisor. He was the authorized school music teacher. The Boston school board report of 1838 distinctly stated that music teaching shall be under the supervision of the

[9] Birge, *History of Public School Music*, p. 49.
[10] *Ibid.*, p. 54.
[11] *Ibid.*, p. 65.

sub-committee of the board. The evolution of the specialist music teacher into the supervisor of music came much later.[12]

The era of the specialist music teacher was actually short lived for:

> The initial system of having children taught entirely by specialized teachers was quickly found to be inadequate. In 1853 in Cleveland, the plan of having children instructed in music by the grade school teachers was started. This necessitated some kind of direction, and the process of music supervision began.[13]

Post-Civil War. The real beginning of music education on any widespread scale in the United States began after the Civil War. Although the work of Lowell Mason, Charles Aiken, Luther Whiting Mason (no relation to Lowell Mason) and others was of great importance, they were trailbreaking pioneers. Their work was confined almost entirely to the big city systems.

School music was heavily influenced by the German tradition but some uniquely American music such as spirituals, the songs of Stephen Foster, and patriotic songs of the Civil War began to be heard in the classroom. However, a correct but anemic music literature was created especially for school use. Tradition dies hard and the not-quite-of-this-world quality still persists with some of our school music today.

About 1870 several "new" subjects in addition to music were introduced in the public school curriculum: manual training, drawing, and physical education. They were usually taught by specialist teachers although in a number of school systems they were taught by the regular teacher with the assistance and support of a specialist. As we have already indicated, in this way specialists came to be called supervisors.

A statement of the period that has quite a familiar ring is this one:

> But in the two decades following the Civil War the relations of the grade teacher to music teaching was by no means clear. Many felt that they should not be asked to teach music and that it was an act of grace on their part to do so. They share the rather common feeling that this was the business of the special music teachers.[14]

The year 1870 also marks the date of the publication of the first series of music books intended to be used progressively through the grades. The *National Music Course* was compiled and edited by Luther Whiting Mason. It was oriented toward the German tradition.

---

[12] *Ibid.*, p. 70.

[13] *Music Supervision and Administration in the Schools* (Chicago: The Music Educators National Conference, 1949), p. 4.

[14] Birge, *History of Public School Music*, p. 104.

It would be inaccurate to give the impression that music education was widely accepted. Music and art, without question, were fringe subjects in a culture that glorified success in the business world. "As late as 1886, General John Eaton, U.S. Commissioner of Education, reported that less than 250 school systems were regularly taking music."[15] Music education was largely in the hands of professional musicians who were not trained in teaching. European traditions in materials and procedures were much in evidence.

Between 1886 and 1889 there was a sudden spurt as a gain of 33 per cent was reported in the number of school systems employing music teachers.[16] Normal schools in their one or two year programs began to provide for the training of elementary music specialists. All of the basic ingredients for American music education were now present. As Britton summarizes it:

> By the year 1900, all of the basic elements of the present system had been laid down. A body of school music teachers existed, together with a textbook literature, a system of teacher training, and a methodology.[17]

Music education was ready for the promise of the new century.

The Twentieth Century

It is well to point out that all of the developments in school music sketched thus far were in the area of vocal music or basic classroom music. There was not much development of instrumental music during the nineteenth century because nearly all of the specialists were vocal music teachers. There were a few school orchestras but they were isolated and experimental. It must also be remembered that the gains were made almost entirely at the elementary level because the American high school did not begin to appear in large numbers until the turn of the century. High school music is almost entirely a development of the twentieth century.

Since 1900 the schools of the United States have been engaged in the world's first truly democratic experiment in music education. No other country has even attempted to provide musical opportunities for all children as a part of their basic, general education. Even in European countries such as Germany the appreciation of music and skill in amateur performance have been fostered more in individual homes than in the schools. Nowhere, except perhaps in England, have schools considered offering music to all of the children of all of the people part of their normal function.

Educational psychology of the first two decades of the century was characterized by Herbartian pedagogy with its emphasis on detailed lesson

---

[15] *Ibid.*, p. 82.
[16] *Ibid.*, p. 110.
[17] Britton, "Music Education: An American Specialty," p. 29.

plans and definitive procedures as well as early evidences of the child study movement. The old and new approaches might be contrasted in this way:

Old	*New*
Authority imposed from above.	Individuality encouraged.
External discipline.	Self-discipline.
Learning from texts.	Learning through experience.
Acquisition of skills and techniques by drill.	Acquisition of skills as a means to an end.
Preparation for a more or less remote future.	Making the most of the present.
Static aims and outlook.	Concept of a changing world.
Stiff environment, fixed desks.	Informal, cheerful environment.
Pre-conceived courses of study.	Timing of subject offerings with the growth and development of children.
The school as an isolated social institution.	The school as a part of the larger community.

The impact of the new philosophy had a positive influence on music education. It not only justified its place in the curriculum but it also gave music a more important role. Music was no longer regarded as something nice-but-unnecessary, something of pleasure but of dubious value. It became, instead, a unique and important experience in the development of the child. We are still a long way from a complete acceptance of this ideal but the work of John Dewey, William James, and Charles Pierce was of great value to music education.

Another important turn of the century development was the growing recognition of music education as a profession within the broad field of music. Music education began to find its place slowly but surely among the established areas of music study such as applied music, theory, composition, conducting, and musicology. This growing professionalism was marked by the birth of a professional organization, the *Music Supervisors Conference*. This organization had its beginning when 104 people interested in school music gathered in Keokuk, Iowa, for a three-day meeting, April 10–12, 1907. In 1910 the name was changed to the *Music Supervisors National Conference* and in 1934 to the *Music Educators National Conference*.

It is interesting to note in the light of what has gone before and what is yet to come that the very first program of the *Music Supervisors Conference* on Friday, April 10, 1907 included the topic "What Teachers Can Do with Voice Training in the Primary Grades."[18] Although a topic on the elementary teacher and music teaching might be rephrased in a current convention, it is still a popular and lively one.

[18] Lilla Belle Pitts, *News Release for the Golden Anniversary Commission* (Washington: The Music Educators National Conference, January, 1957).

This Keokuk meeting was important because from it emerged a professional, voluntary, non-governmental association of music teachers. It provided unity and authority within the profession. It is now the recognized spokesman for music education in this country.

It was about 1910 that the first school bands began to appear. Unlike the earlier orchestras which were comprised of students who were already studying privately, the band was developed within the school itself. For instrumental music education, this was an innovation of major import.

In the Twenties instructional supervision was regarded by most educators as a directing, telling, and checking procedure. The typical supervisor of instruction may have been benevolent but he was a benevolent autocrat. The idea of supervision as a cooperative, democratic process was yet to come. However, in the Twenties, the influence of the child-centered philosophy was making itself increasingly evident. The expressive subjects such as music and art were seen in a favorable light by most educators. Special supervisors of art, music, and physical education in cities with a population of more than 100,000 were quite common. Many smaller systems followed suit. However, in some situations there was a reaction against specialist supervisors on the ground that the specialist tended to overemphasize his special interest area. Many school administrators felt that supervision should be entrusted only to general supervisors and building principals.

The Thirties was the period of the depression. Resistance to special supervisors was intensified by a shortage of funds. A curtailment of the music program was the norm in those places where music instruction was regarded as a "frill." There was a sharp de-emphasis on music reading and the social studies oriented music program became firmly established. Extra-musical or extrinsic values were emphasized in music education.

This decade also saw the emergence of "democratic" supervision. However, it was found more in professional writing than in actual practice. Speaking of democratic supervision, Wiles has this comment:

> But a survey of the literature reveals that this term meant a type of manipulation in which teachers were to be treated kindly and maneuvered into doing what the supervisor wanted to do all along.[19]

In the Forties the philosophical thinking that was considered controversial at the beginning of the century was widely accepted. "Learning by doing" became a catch-phrase that was used in all educational camps. Writers now referred to supervision as a cooperative rather than a directive endeavor. The general supervisor's role was regarded to be one of assisting and sharing rather than ordering. This shift in philosophy also made its impact on music supervision.

[19] Kimball Wiles, *Supervision for Better Schools* (New York: Prentice-Hall, Inc., 2nd ed., 1955), p. 5.

The shift from autocratic to democratic supervision may be contrasted in this manner:

Autocratic	*Democratic*
Authority is stressed.	Cooperation is stressed.
There are few leaders.	There are many leaders, emergent leadership is encouraged.
Authority is imposed from above.	Strength is derived from below.
Based on stern management.	Based on a concern for human relations.
Standardization is the norm.	Creativity is encouraged.

The music program expanded during the decade but usually at the expense of less and less consultant service. The "self-contained" classroom became the standard and some administrators began to question seriously whether specialists of any kind should be employed at the elementary level. However, Ayer reports: "A 1949 report of the Federal Office of Education indicates the presence in cities of 10,000 and over of practically as many specialist supervisors, especially in art, music, and physical education as were employed in former years."[20]

By mid-century there was a growing conviction that music had something to say for itself. Without disparaging the contributions that music had made and was continuing to make as an enrichment subject, leaders in music education were speaking more and more of music as a significant learning in its own right.

It is impossible to pass the year 1957 without commenting on Sputnik and its effect on education. There was a quick retreat from the humanities in many quarters. There was considerable soul-searching and an almost frantic effort to establish new priorities as to what should be taught in the public schools.

However, to the great credit of the overwhelming majority of school administrators, there was no marked de-emphasis of music education. Perhaps this resistance to pressure was nowhere more dramatically exemplified than at the 1959 convention of the American Association of School Administrators in Atlantic City, N.J. All major sessions of the convention were given over to a consideration of the creative, performing arts. In a resolution adopted at the end of the convention, administrators had this to say:

> We believe in a well-balanced school curriculum in which music, drama, painting, poetry, sculpture, architecture, and the like are included side by side with other important subjects such as mathematics, history, and science. It is important that pupils, as a part of general education, learn to appreciate, to understand, to create, and to criticize with discrimination those products of the mind, the voice, the hand,

[20] Fred C. Ayer, *Fundamentals of Instructional Supervision* (New York: Harper & Row, Publishers, 1954), p. 11.

and the body which give dignity to the person and exalt the spirit of man.[21]

Summary

Music teaching goes back to the earliest days of recorded history. The term *music* to the Greeks meant what we would call the arts today. Music was valued for its training of the soul. Gymnastics was important for the training of the body.

In Rome music was considered one of the seven liberal arts. These arts included grammar, rhetoric, and logic (the *trivium*) and arithmetic, geometry, astronomy, and music (the *quadrivium*).

In the Middle Ages music was still regarded more as an intellectual pursuit than a performing art. A body of music theory came into being. Music was a part of the curriculum in the cathedral schools and the palace schools. The peasants learned about music in the home or from wandering minstrels.

In the Renaissance music was valued for its performance even more than for its theoretical study. Music instruction was standard in the schools of the church and the court. The educational ideal was the "well rounded" man.

The Reformation gave great impetus to music education. Vernacular schools and the invention of printing made learning possible for more and more people.

In North America, there were evidences of music instruction in Mexico and the area we now know as New Mexico as early as the sixteenth century. Music education in colonial New England was minimal. Most of the early colonists had little time to devote to the arts.

The singing school was a major force in music education in America. Some of our earliest composers were singing school masters and one of them, Lowell Mason, inaugurated the first public school program in Boston in 1838. The early school music programs were actually transplanted singing schools.

After the Civil War, music education developed rapidly in all parts of the country. At the end of the century we had the basic elements of elementary music education: teachers, teacher-training institutions, music textbooks, and a methodology.

In the twentieth century, new philosophical concepts aided the growth of music education. Music education gained status as a profession. Democratic supervision came to be a goal in music education as well as in general education. Despite setbacks of the depression years and the first reactions following the launching of Sputnik, American school administrators went on record in 1959 as endorsing the necessity for including music in a well-balanced curriculum.

Questions for Discussion

1. What did the word *music* mean in the education of Greek youth?
2. Discuss the place of music as one of the seven liberal arts.
3. Describe the singing school movement. What was its influence on early music education in America?
4. Investigate further the principles of Johann Pestalozzi and their influence on music teaching. Do these principles still have application today?

[21] Quoted by Finis Engleman, Executive Secretary, American Association of School Administrators in "Music and Public Education," *The Music Educators Journal,* February–March, 1961, p. 36.

5. Granting that it is quite possible that Lowell Mason was not the very first school music teacher, what was the particular significance of his work in Boston?

6. Do you think that the German tradition still dominates the school music series? Investigate several of them and report your findings.

7. Were the first teachers of music in the elementary schools specialists or classroom teachers? Has the issue finally been resolved as to who should teach music in the elementary school?

8. How do you react to the statement that a "correct but anemic" literature was created especially for school use in the nineteenth century? Is the statement applicable to any degree today?

9. Contrast the "old" and the "new" educational philosophies that were current at the turn of the century.

10. What is meant by the term "democratic supervision"?

15

Current Practice

Although men in every era undoubtedly felt that they lived in changing times, it seems that we live in a world of change of sweeping proportions. One has only to consider the changes that have taken place in transportation within our generation to realize how true this is. Break-throughs in science and technology have also brought dramatic changes. Educators, too, are caught up in changes occurring so rapidly that it seems impossible for the professional to keep informed of new developments.

Music education is also changing. The place that music holds in the curriculum reflects the position it holds in American life. We would certainly be exaggerating if we said that music now occupies the place in America that it once held in ancient Greece. However, interest in music measured by such yardsticks as sales of records, attendance at concerts, and the number of civic symphonies is reassuring. School music is holding its own and, in many quarters, is making substantial gains.

Howerton summarizes the situation very well:

It is unfortunately true that until more or less recently the field of music has been dominated by an essentially nineteenth century concept, which is to say, regarded as a pleasant adornment, a delightful pastime for those with little else to occupy their idle moments, a status symbol evidencing financial success or social prestige, but often incomprehended as one of the vital expressions of man's inner spirit, one of the essences of which his soul is compounded. There is happily observable today a

172

change in the current, and music is once more properly assuming its ancient position as one of the honorable disciplines.[1]

Generalizations Based on the Past

A number of generalizations may be drawn from our historical review of music education. They are:

1. Instruction in music in the elementary school has a long tradition. It is now well established in the elementary program of the American school.

2. Music education has been subject to the stresses of "the times" throughout its history. From Plato, who was impressed with the mathematical marvel of tonal relationships, to the impact created by the launching of orbiting satellites, music teaching has been directly affected by contemporary forces.

3. There has been a strong influence of the church on music teaching. Music's status in the Middle Ages and the Reformation was due in large part to the needs of the church. The American singing schools had as their major objectives the improvement of church choirs and congregational singing. The tradition continues with many music educators serving in a dual capacity as school and church musicians.

4. The emphasis given in music education to extrinsic or extra-musical values by laymen as well as educators has persisted since the earliest days of music teaching.

5. Although early leaders in music education from the first advocated the teaching of music for its intrinsic values, the evolutionary process from music as a recreational pursuit, to social studies enrichment, to an aesthetic discipline has been a long, slow one.

6. From the earliest period of music education in America, there has been considerable confusion as to who should teach music in the elementary school: the elementary teacher or the elementary music specialist. The issue is by no means resolved.

7. The development of the principles of democratic supervision in general education has had a direct influence on the work of the elementary music specialist and the supervisor of music. Elementary music supervision is now regarded as a cooperative, sharing endeavor rather than a tutorial process.

8. Music education has not always been in the mainstream of American music. For example, in the nineteenth century the vigorous music of Billings and Hopkinson was largely ignored in preference to a much more bland, "pretty" kind of music. Happily, this preoccupation with a correct but colorless "school music" literature is giving way to music of greater virility and integrity.

[1] George Howerton, "Music as One of the Humanities," *Music Educators Journal,* Sept.–Oct., 1962, p. 28.

Current Status

What is the current status of music in the elementary school? Without attempting to be facetious, it depends upon whom you ask. Nye and Nye have this to say:

> While some believe that the quality of music teaching has improved, and that teachers of music are better prepared for their work than in earlier years, others are convinced that the opposite is true, and claim that the situation in most elementary classrooms today is reminiscent of that of from forty to fifty years ago.[2]

How can this be? One has only to take a casual look at current practice to see how widely divergent it is. It is possible to have one school system with a superior music program in elementary music education located immediately adjacent to another school system that has none.

The following appraisal of current practice is drawn from three studies, two undertaken by the writer and a third by the Research Division of the National Education Association. A state-wide study[3] was conducted in 1960 and a regional study[4] of thirteen states was made in 1962. The national study[5] was reported in 1963.

In the studies undertaken by the writer, music specialists were queried regarding *current* practice. At the same time, they were asked for suggestions concerning *recommended* practice. Since the study for the thirteen states represents a wider sampling over a larger geographical area, the figures are reported from the regional study. However, it is interesting to point out that the responses made in depth in one state (every elementary music specialist was queried) to one of breadth in thirteen states (a cross-section of elementary music specialists was selected by the state supervisor of music) are so closely parallel as to give validity to the studies. Ninety-seven replies were received in the state study, and 201 replies were received in the regional study.

Regional Study

1. *Functions of the elementary music specialist.* Music specialists were

[2] Robert E. Nye and Vernice T. Nye, *Music in the Elementary School,* 2nd ed. (Englewood Cliffs, New Jersey: Prentice-Hall, Inc., 1964), pp. 1–2.

[3] *Consultant Practices in Elementary Music Education* (Baton Rouge, La.: Louisiana State Department of Education, 1960).

[4] "Current and Recommended Practices in Elementary Music Supervision." A report made by the writer as chairman of the Committee on Supervision, Administration, and Curriculum Development for the Southern Music Educators Conference, Charlotte, West Virginia, 1963.

[5] *Music and Art in the Public Schools* (Washington, D.C.: Research Division, National Education Association, Monograph 1963-M3, 1963).

asked to select between two choices: "Do you consider your role to be (1) that of a consultant, that is, helping elementary teachers become more effective in teaching music in their classes, or (2) serving as the music teacher, that is, most or all of the music teaching is done by the specialist?"[6]

77 indicated that they were music consultants.
118 indicated that they served as music teachers.

When the same questions were put in terms of recommended practice:

133 indicated that they preferred to serve as music consultants.
 58 preferred to work as music teachers.

There is an obvious disparity in the way things are and the way music specialists would like them to be. From the study, it is clear that most elementary music specialists are working as music teachers rather than as consultants. Most would prefer to work as consultants.

2. *Focus of music teaching.* A second question asked was in regard to the focus or emphasis given to the manner in which music is taught: "Do you feel that music is taught as a significant learning in its own right or as an enrichment subject?" In responding:

33 indicated that music was taught primarily as a significant learning in its own right.
43 indicated that music was taught primarily as an enrichment subject.
124 indicated that equal emphasis was given to both alternatives.

In answer to the same question concerning recommended practice:

33 indicated that music should be taught primarily as a discipline in its own right.
 9 indicated that music should be taught primarily as an enrichment subject.
158 indicated that music should be taught with equal emphasis on both points.

From the responses, it is clear that the majority feel that this is not an either-or choice, that both the extrinsic as well as the intrinsic values need to be emphasized. The significant difference in recommended practice is the reduction in the number who feel that music should be taught as an enrichment subject. However, the number who believe music should be taught as a significant learning did not change at all. The emphasis given to the teaching of music as an aesthetic discipline is much more evident in professional writing than it is in actual practice.

3. *Number of teachers served.* Another point of inquiry in the study was the number of teachers served by each specialist. Admittedly, this is a difficult question on which to draw conclusions because of the many variables involved. The working role of the specialist, the size of schools, the curriculum policy concerning the responsibility of elementary teachers to teach

---

[6] Since not all respondents answered all questions, total responses are less than 201.

music, the frequency of visits, and travel distances involved are all important factors.

In answer to the question: "How many elementary teachers do you serve?" the responses were distributed as indicated on Graph No. 1. The number of respondents answering is reported vertically, the number of teachers served is reported horizontally. Current practice is indicated by the heavy line while recommended practice is indicated by the light line. The dots at the figure 100 indicate that there were individual respondents who served more than 100 teachers. One respondent served 500 elementary teachers. Comments made by respondents serving more than 100 teachers indicated that they were supervisors of music with very broad responsibilities in music education.

GRAPH 1

NUMBER OF CLASSROOM TEACHERS
SERVED BY ONE MUSIC CONSULTANT

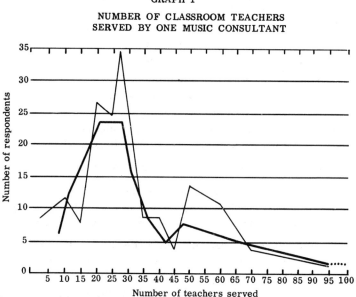

In both current and recommended practice the study reveals that most specialists serve from 25 to 30 classroom teachers. This is one of the most important findings of the study.

4. *Number of daily classroom visits.* Another item that was investigated was the number of classroom visits that each specialist scheduled in one day. The figures reported indicate the number of classroom visits made or the number of comparable services performed. If a specialist visits eight different classrooms, the figure eight is reported. If she visits six classes, conducts the elementary chorus for one-half hour, and works for one-half hour with several third-grade classes in the auditorium, the figure eight is also reported.

As in Graph No. 1, on Graph No. 2 current practice is indicated by a heavy line, recommended practice by a light line. The number of respondents is reported vertically, the number of classrooms visited is indicated horizontally. No respondent visited more than fifteen classrooms daily.

GRAPH 2

NUMBER OF CLASSROOMS VISITED
DAILY BY ONE MUSIC CONSULTANT

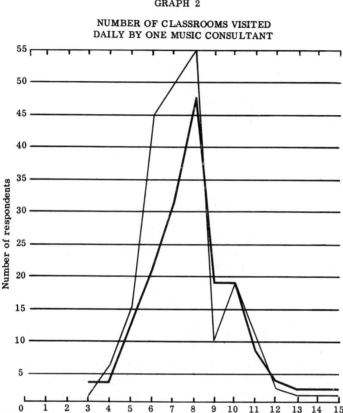

Number of daily classroom visits

Again, it is quite clear that current and recommended practice are closely parallel. Fifty respondents indicated that they serve eight classrooms in one day. Fifty-five specialists recommend this as the optimum number of visits for an ideal working schedule.

5. *Preparing the specialist's schedule.* In actual practice, 60 per cent of the respondents made out their schedules cooperatively with teachers and principals. Other specialists prepared their schedules alone, with the supervisor of music, or with the assistance of the general supervisor of instruction. In terms of recommended practice, 70 per cent believe it desirable for the specialist, the principal, and teachers to prepare the schedule cooperatively.

6. *Title.* In answer to the question, "What is your working title?" the respondents answered as follows:

Title	Respondents
Elementary Music Teacher	71
Elementary Music Supervisor	47
Elementary Music Consultant	23
Helping Music Teacher	11
Public School Music Teacher	10
Director of Music	9
Elementary Vocal Teacher	7
Elementary Music Specialist	7
Elementary Music Resource Teacher	5
Coordinator of Music	4
Elementary Music Instructor	3
Itinerant Music Teacher	1

In recommending a working title respondents answered as follows:

Title	Respondents
Elementary Music Consultant	50
Elementary Music Teacher	29
Elementary Music Supervisor	26
Elementary Music Specialist	20
Elementary Music Resource Teacher	10
Helping Music Teacher	10
Director of Music	8
Elementary Music Instructor	5
Coordinator of Music	3
Public School Music Teacher	3
Elementary Vocal Teacher	2

It is interesting to note that some 25 per cent recommend the title *music consultant*. This is in line with the specialist's feelings as to her preferred role as a helping, consultant teacher rather than as the direct music teacher.

7. *In-service education.* In answer to the question: "Do you believe in-service meetings for teachers should be included as a part of your work?":

82 indicated that they conducted in-service meetings.
114 indicated that they did not.

However, in regard to recommended practice:

164 believed that they should conduct in-service meetings.
26 felt that they should not.

Apparently, music specialists feel that in-service sessions are highly desirable. However, according to this study, only about 40 per cent of the music specialists actually conduct them.

8. *Expressed concerns.* In addition to these responses, specialists were also asked to indicate three topics of major concern. As was expected, a very large number of concerns were expressed. By grouping similar responses into

categories, some sixty-one topics were listed in the report. Common concerns in order of frequency are summarized below:

33 responses   Developing a positive attitude toward music on the part of the elementary teacher.

25–30 responses   Determining who is responsible for teaching music in the elementary program.
                    Deciding what emphasis to give to the teaching of music reading, discovering effective ways of teaching music reading, establishing reasonable goals for music reading.
                    Increasing the status of music in the elementary program.

20–24 responses   Defining the role of the elementary music specialist.
                    Developing effective in-service procedures.
                    Implementing curriculum development.
                    Establishing grade level musical goals.

15–19 responses   Strengthening college music education courses, making college courses more functional.
                    Scheduling the work of the elementary music specialist within the school.
                    Establishing the number of schools assigned to one music specialist, establishing the number of teachers to be served.
                    Obtaining the interest and support of principals and administrators.

10–14 responses   Clarifying the relationships between the specialist and elementary teachers.
                    Obtaining financial support for elementary music.
                    Developing a listening program.
                    Determining the place of instrumental music in the elementary school.

State Study

In the state-wide study, in addition to the statistical information gathered, a "feeling tone" was obtained by inviting short comments from music specialists. Since these comments add an affective reaction that the statistical figures lack, the following quotations have been selected as representative from the hundreds offered. They strengthen and color the expressed concerns cited above.

In response to the question: "In what respects are you *most* satisfied with the program as it is now operating?" these comments were made:

The children's enjoyment and enthusiastic participation.

The children love music. They are interested and responsive and we get pleasing results.

I have two thirty minute periods for each classroom every week. The children are showing progress in note reading. All seem to look forward to my coming.

The satisfaction of aiding teachers in developing an appreciation of music.

The teachers are assuming more and more responsibility. Excellent cooperation is given by my principals.

My schedule at each school runs smoothly and in most cases the classroom teachers are cooperative.

The new music material is an inspiration.

We have record players in every room.

For a small school offering many subjects, I believe adequate time is given to music teaching.

In response to the question: "In what respects are you *least* satisfied with the music program as it is now operating?" these comments were made:

Music is not an integral part of the school program.

I feel that the principal should be the head of his school and promote or foster all subjects. My principal does not evidence an active interest in the music program.

Music is scheduled as an activity rather than a subject. I have a feeling that the children think of my time with them as entertainment or a recreation period.

I feel that the greatest need is for a broad understanding of the purpose of music in the elementary school. There is a need for someone to coordinate and supervise the program.

Teachers do not stay in the classroom during my visit.

Teachers expect the specialist to do the teaching of music. Our teachers do not have sufficient "know how" to carry on the program.

I do not have enough time to be a resource person or offer real help when a teacher needs it. Most of the music period is spent in singing. Rhythm, creative expression, listening, playing instruments, and note reading are neglected.

To meet all teachers once a week, three classes are grouped together in the auditorium. This is assembly singing, not classroom teaching!

I travel almost as much as I teach.

Special programs take too much time.

I am tired of our old music books.

In response to the question: "What specific suggestions do you have to *improve* the program of music education in the elementary schools?" these responses were made:

More pre-service training for elementary teachers. I believe that if student teachers in college were impressed with the importance of music in the classroom they would do a better job.

Most of our teachers were not asked to teach music in their practice teaching. They soon get the idea that music teaching is not an important responsibility.

We need more realistic training of music specialists. No one ever gave me suggestions on how to get the classroom teacher to "take over."

Clarification of the music specialist's role by the central office. The administration does not always have a clear idea as to why we have a music program. They hire specialists because the classroom teachers ask for them.

We need more workshops and informal group discussions with elementary teachers.

I think a better understanding is needed between teachers and music specialists. I fail here more than in any other one thing.

Require the classroom teacher to stay in the room during the music period. If we could bring classroom teachers to the realization that music classes are of importance and not rest periods, greater goals could be achieved.

If principals and administrators could make the teachers feel responsible for teaching music half of our problems would be solved. We not only demonstrate how to teach music but we have to "sell" teachers on the importance of including music in their teaching schedule.

I would like fewer assigned classrooms. We need more specialists to do an effective job. We should visit each teacher twice a week.

National Study

The national study conducted by the Research Division of the National Education Association, *Music and Art in the Public Schools,* is one of the most thorough and far-reaching studies made in the field of music education for many years. It reveals many significant facts concerning the current status of elementary education.

Questionnaires were mailed to 790 elementary school principals selected by random procedures in such a way as to obtain a representative sampling of schools in all possible classifications. The report is based on 657 replies received. These are some of the findings as they apply to elementary music education:

1. The trend is toward more music in the elementary school rather than less. Ninety-seven per cent of elementary schools now offer some type of formal or informal instruction in music.

2. Although music is offered in nearly all schools, it is scheduled for less time during the week than the minimum standards recommended by the Music Educators National Conference. The MENC recommendation is 100 minutes per week for grades 1 to 3 and 125 to 150 minutes per week for grades 4 to 6. The median time allotment of schools participating in the study was slightly less than 80 minutes per week.

3. Although music was definitely scheduled in nearly two-thirds of the participating schools, only half of these schools had a definite course of study.

4. Concerning the question of who teaches music (elementary teacher alone, specialist alone, or a combination of both teacher and specialist),

forty per cent of the schools reported the use of the cooperative approach. The breakdown for grade levels is as follows:[7]

Grade	No formal instruction	Classroom teacher only	Classroom teacher with help from specialist	Specialist only	No reply	Total
1	5.0%	40.5%	40.2%	12.6%	1.7%	100%
2	5.5	39.0	40.7	13.4	1.4	100
3	5.0	37.0	41.1	15.5	1.4	100
4	5.9	31.6	40.7	20.4	1.4	100
5	5.8	30.3	40.3	22.1	1.5	100
6	6.1	30.5	38.3	23.2	1.9	100

In other words, in three-fourths of the elementary schools in the United States the elementary teacher is responsible for some or all of the music program. She is given varying degrees of help by the elementary music specialist.

5. Schools in large school districts are more likely to have elementary music programs of high quality than schools having small enrollments. The greatest difference between large districts and small districts was in the percentage of schools having no formal instruction in music.

6. Since classroom teachers are expected to teach music in seventy-five per cent of elementary schools, it would seem reasonable to assume that proficiency in teaching music is a requirement of employment. However, in sixty-three per cent of the schools queried, there was no such requirement. This is one of our most serious problems.

Although many other interesting facts are reported in this national study, these are most pertinent to our investigation of the current status of music education in the elementary school.

Conclusions and Recommendations

As we know, there are many variations in the programs of elementary music education in America. Out of the vast array of facts, opinions, and approaches in current use a number of recurring patterns emerge from which the following *conclusions* are drawn:

1. That most schools use the cooperative approach with the teacher, the specialist, and the principal teaming up to provide music instruction in the elementary classroom.

2. That more elementary music specialists are working as music teachers than as music consultants. Most specialists would prefer to work as consultants.

3. That there is a growing concern to consider music as a significant

[7] *Music and Art in the Public Schools,* p. 15.

learning and an aesthetic discipline. The concept of music's role as entertainment, recreation, and enrichment is taking a subordinate position.

4. That with the increased attention to the study of music *per se,* there is a growing feeling that there should be more structure and more substance in the elementary music program. The program should take into account the developmental characteristics of children.

5. That the biggest problem is not the curriculum so much as its implementation. We know a great deal more of what we ought to be doing than what we are actually doing.

In the light of the findings of the studies, personal experience, and the collective thinking of many professional associates, the writer feels it is in order to make the following *recommendations* concerning current status:

1. That the role of the elementary music specialist in each working situation must be clearly defined. This definition must be made by all concerned and clearly understood by all concerned: specialists, elementary teachers, principals, and administrators. The primary orientation of the music specialist should be as a music consultant.

2. That the elementary teacher, the elementary principal, and the elementary music specialist must accept a *shared* responsibility for the teaching of music. The elementary teacher is the central figure in teaching elementary music.

3. That the emphasis given to the study of music as a significant learning must be given every possible reenforcement. This emphasis places great responsibility on the music specialist to plan and carry out an effective program. More rather than less specialist help is required.

4. That one of the most critical considerations in establishing the schedule of the specialist is the number of classroom visits or services she may perform in one day. An ideal number is eight. The number should not exceed ten.

5. That if the figure of eight services per day is valid, it is obvious that the specialist cannot schedule more than forty visits each week. This means that if the music supervision program is based on the assumption that teachers should be visited *at least* once a week, the specialist cannot possibly serve more than forty teachers. With time needed for travel, for conferences, and additional "on call" requests, the recommended maximum number is thirty elementary teachers for each specialist on a one visit per week basis.

6. That thirty minutes for each visit appears to be practical and effective. This is one point on which there is almost unanimous agreement in the studies.

7. That the prevailing practice of preparing a visitation schedule for the specialist with teachers and the principal is a good one and should be continued. The determining question is: "How can we use the services of the music specialist to the best possible advantage?" It is not the most effective plan to divide mathematically the available time of the specialist among the

teachers to be served. The schedule must be adjusted from time to time to take care of changing needs.

8. That administrative expectation concerning music teaching in the elementary program cannot be overemphasized. In this regard the principal plays a key role.

9. That one of the most serious shortcomings is the lack of adequate provision for in-service education on the job. It is a procedure that holds great promise for the improvement of instruction. Every music specialist should consider in-service group study as much a part of her work as class-room visitation.

10. That if the teaching of music in the classroom is an expected part of the elementary teacher's responsibility, then proficiency in music teaching should be a requisite for employment. More and better college preparation is required and practice teaching must include experiences in music education.

One of the more disturbing fallacies held by many general educators concerning the elementary music specialist is that she is so concerned and involved with music as a special interest that she is quite insensitive to the needs of children. Although music educators do need to utilize the findings of developmental psychologists to a greater degree, the elementary music specialist has the opportunity to observe children in widely varied situations. In many ways, the specialist is in a unique position to study behavioral patterns of boys and girls in all of the elementary grades.

Another disturbing fallacy is one held by many music specialists that the great majority of elementary teachers cannot teach music. One of our most pressing problems is for specialists to learn how to work more effectively in a consultant role with elementary teachers. It takes an extremely skillful, sensitive music specialist to work cooperatively with teachers to develop and improve a program. It is much easier for the specialist to "take charge" than it is to help the teacher become more effective in her own music teaching. Without question, it is more difficult to serve as a music consultant than as a music teacher. We must improve our consultant practices.

Summary

Music education, like other aspects of American life, is changing rapidly. Drawing from the historical past, we know that there has long been an emphasis on extra-musical or extrinsic aspects of music teaching rather than on music's unique and intrinsic values. Happily, we are moving once more in the direction of considering music as one of the honorable disciplines.

In regard to current status, an overview of present practice was made on the basis of three studies: (1) a state-wide study, (2) a regional study including thirteen states, and (3) a national study.

Reactions from several hundred music educators were received in the state and regional studies concerning the role of the elementary music specialist, the status of music in the elementary curriculum, and the working schedule of the specialist. Reactions included both current practice and recommended practice. The major problems or concerns of elementary music specialists were identified.

In the national study, evidence gathered indicates that there is a trend toward more music in the elementary school. However, many schools are providing less than a minimum program in terms of scheduled time. In three-fourths of the elementary schools participating in this study the elementary teacher is responsible for some or all of the music program. She receives varying degrees of assistance from the music specialist. Although elementary teachers are expected to teach music, proficiency in music teaching is generally not a requirement for employment.

In drawing his own conclusions regarding current practice, the writer feels that the cooperative approach involving specialist, teacher, and principal is used in most elementary schools, that music specialists are working more as music teachers than consultants, that specialists would prefer to work as consultants, that there is a growing concern to emphasize music as an aesthetic experience, and that the big problem is not the curriculum so much as its implementation.

Recommendations include a continuing need to clarify the role of the specialist, to reenforce the concept of music as a significant learning, to establish eight to ten visits daily as a reasonable schedule for the consultant, to establish a maximum of thirty to forty teachers on a one visit per week basis for each consultant, to emphasize administrative expectancy concerning music teaching in the elementary school, and to foster in-service education.

Questions for Discussion

1. Why do you suppose that there has been such a consistent emphasis on extramusical or extrinsic values in music education throughout its history? Do you see evidences of a shift to a greater concern for intrinsic values?

2. What is your own opinion about the current status of elementary music education?

3. Discuss this statement: "The emphasis given to the teaching of music as an aesthetic discipline is much more evident in professional writing than it is in actual practice."

4. Why is the number of services or supervisory visits that the consultant can complete in one day such a critical figure?

5. If elementary music specialists consider in-service education so important, why do less than half of them actually conduct in-service study groups?

6. Why is "developing a positive attitude toward music on the part of the elementary teacher" at the top of the list of expressed concerns of music specialists?

7. The fact that in three-fourths of the elementary schools of the United States the elementary teacher is responsible for some or all of the music program suggests many things to music educators. Discuss.

8. What is meant by the statement: "The biggest problem is not the curriculum so much as its implementation"?

9. What changes would you recommend in the undergraduate preparation of prospective elementary teachers to teach music?

10. How would you define the working role of the elementary music specialist? How do you believe she should function?

16

What Lies Ahead?

Following our historical review and our examination of current practice, it seems in order to consider future trends. We have looked backward to where we have been, we have taken stock as to where we are, and we would like very much to know where we are going.

A number of trends in elementary education are having a direct effect on music education. Many groups (including music educators) are seeking more time in the elementary program. There are pressures to intensify the "academic" areas. In almost all subjects grade-level expectancies are being moved downward; that is, we now expect fourth grade children to do many of the things that were formerly assigned to grade five or six. Grade level lines are less sacred. Experimentation is under way to group on the basis of learning ability rather than chronological age. There is a renewed emphasis on action research as a basis for curriculum construction. Team-teaching, educational television, and programmed learning are in the present picture and they will assume increasingly important roles in the future. The most significant trend is an increased expectancy for improved learning experiences and for quality teaching.

Future Implications for Music Education

What are the implications for music education? What is our direction for the future? Although it is highly presumptuous to attempt any "crystal ball" gazing, there are a number of evolving trends that point very strongly to future developments.

1. There is a strong trend toward improved *musical* experiences at the elementary level. The emphasis has already shifted from an elementary music program that is social-studies-oriented to one that is music-centered. In our search for improved quality, we must emphasize in every possible way the study of music as a discipline, as a significant learning, as an art, as an aesthetic.

Perhaps this shifting emphasis is nowhere more obvious than in a comparative study of basic elementary music series. The tables of contents have changed from such titles as "Singing Along the Highway" to such categories as "Form in Music" and "Creating Music." The correlation and enrichment values of music are important but we are finally facing up to them for what they are: extrinsic values that must be considered in second place to intrinsic values. In a social-studies-oriented unit we may have a category such as "Ways of Going Places" (primary grades) or "Transportation" (intermediate grades). In this unit we may have several good songs about ships, about trains, and about horses but none at all about automobiles. When we find an automobile song, even one of little musical worth, we seize upon it enthusiastically. A possibility for correlated enrichment should not justify the use of a shoddy piece of music. Musical values should not be subordinated to correlation values.

Our new frontier in elementary music education, then, is to develop musical quality. Most of us have at least minimal time for music activities. Our greatest problem is not to get more time, as desirable as this may be, but to fill the time we already have with better music and better experiences for boys and girls.

2. There is a need to make music a more integral part of the elementary program. It would seem that every music educator would be vitally concerned in seeing to it that music is or becomes an integral part of general education. However, when opportunities present themselves to move in this direction, we are too often our own worst enemies. Music educators, by and large, often think of music concerns as so specialized as to be beyond the ken of teachers of other subjects, principals, and administrators. The technical language of music is complex and involved, but the relationship of music to the overall program is sometimes seen more clearly by general educators than by music educators.

Fortunately, at the elementary level, music is widely accepted for its contribution to the growth and development of children. We speak hopefully of an expanded program of general music at the secondary level but nowhere do we approach the goal of music for all children as well as we do in the elementary school.

The public relations emphasis that is so often over-emphasized in junior and senior high school is held to a minimum at the elementary level. We must be on our guard to maintain the primary focus on what music can do for children. Beware when someone begins to talk about performances to "sell" the elementary program, or about a fund-raising campaign to uniform the second grade rhythm band, or about the elementary band "putting on a little show" for the next inter-school football game.

Let us be sure that we emphasize the musical rather than the extra-musical aspects of elementary school music. Only in this way can we hope to make music an integral part of the curriculum.

3. There is a need to understand more clearly the contributions music can make to personality fulfillment. Planning, implementing, and carrying on a program of elementary music must be made not only in terms of desired musical learnings but also with a due regard for the developmental readiness of boys and girls. This means that we cannot take the total learnings to be accomplished in the elementary program and divide them into six neat packages, one package for each grade.

To plan offerings for the third grade, for example, we must know a great deal about eight and nine year olds before we can provide appropriate experiences. In planning a sequential elementary music program we must not only have a clear idea of the body of information and skills we hope to impart but we must also have a good understanding of the interests, capabilities, and limitations of boys and girls at each chronological level.

In music education we have done little more than to scratch the surface in capitalizing on the principles of child growth and development. We need to do much more in relating the findings of developmental psychology to the teaching of music.

Continuing Need for Specialist Help

In regard to the services of the elementary music consultant, the following observations appear to be in order: (1) Elementary teachers want and will continue to need consultant help in teaching music; (2) Principals and administrators generally recognize the need for consultant help at the elementary level; and (3) Parents expect musical experiences for their boys and girls in the elementary school.

1. *Elementary teachers need consultant help.* The biggest single reason why consultants are employed in elementary schools is because teachers have consistently indicated a need for their services. Two other areas where specialist help is often requested are art and physical education.

Ayer supports this contention in his list of needs of teachers as a basis for a supervisory program. Heading his list of teacher needs is "the need for better techniques and methods of teaching special skills, especially in reading, social studies, music and art."[1] Replogle also supports this point in his article entitled "What Help Do Teachers Want?" He states that one of the commonly cited needs is "using art and music to better advantage in the regular classroom situation."[2]

With the strong trend toward emphasizing musical values there is little reason to question the need for the services of the elementary music consultant. The average teacher requires the guidance and help of the specialist both in classroom visits and in-service education. If anything, more rather than less specialist help will be required in a program emphasizing musical learnings.

2. *Administrators recognize the need for specialist help.* Although it is generally conceded that teachers need specialist help in the classroom, it is not so generally conceded that the great majority of principals and instructional supervisors are not as confident in supervising the music program as they are in supervising other areas of the elementary curriculum. This does not mean to say that the principal-supervisor has little notion of how the expressive arts should fit into an overall program. What the administrator seeks from the specialist is how the broad, general aims of music education may be translated into a specific day-by-day program.

The administrator can see the broad picture very well. He depends on the music specialist to help him fill in the details. If the principal feels that he can trust the judgment of the specialist to implement the program within the broad outlines established by the philosophy of the school he is only too happy to delegate this responsibility.

However, when the specialist takes the attitude: "Mr. Principal, my subject is so special and so technical that the usual ground rules for supervision do not apply," then there is understandable resistance on his part to delegate authority for curriculum development.

3. *Parents expect music in the elementary curriculum.* Parents and school patrons have the last word as to what the school curriculum includes. A pragmatic question for curriculum workers to consider is: "What do educated parents want in the way of an education for their children?" Parents consider the school in their community as a "good school" when students are not only given adequate experiences in communication skills, in number skills, and in the sciences but also in the expressive arts.

It is largely because of repeated requests by parents that music experiences have been provided in the school curriculum. Far too often, plans for music would have been largely ignored if it were not for the persistent demands of parents.

Increasing attention is being given to the arts in everyday living. In

[1] Fred C. Ayer, *Fundamentals of Instructional Supervision* (New York: Harper & Row, Publishers, 1954), p. 401.
[2] V. L. Replogle, "What Help Do Teachers Want?" *Educational Leadership,* Vol. 7, No. 7, April, 1950, p. 477.

our materialistic, business-dominated society, such a statement may sound like the most idealistic kind of wishful thinking. However, the sales of musical instruments, the explosive development of a wide variety of electronic reproducing equipment, and growing concert audiences are evidences of the important place that music plays in American life. Adults who are becoming increasingly interested in the arts are expecting improved aesthetic experiences for their children in school. So long as parents feel that activities in the arts are not only desirable but essential for the well-rounded development of their children, we shall have music in the programs of the public schools.

Predictable Trends

Current practice points up some predictable trends for elementary music education. Some of the more significant trends are:

1. *Elementary music specialists will achieve improved professional status.* The elementary music specialist of the future will continue to require a broad liberal arts background as well as preparation in basic musicianship and applied music. However, she must be able to see her work more clearly in its relationship to the overall program of elementary education. Administrators will become increasingly concerned about her professional qualifications in elementary education. This does not mean that they will expect her to be an expert in teaching reading or mathematics but they will expect her to be aware of the grade level goals in these areas to the extent that she can relate them to her work in music education.

The elementary music specialist will receive more professional recognition in the field of music education. Most prospective music teachers would like to teach either at the secondary or the college level. To many students, the elementary level is not particularly attractive. The truth of the matter is that in terms of shaping the course of music education and, more important, in influencing the lives of children, the elementary level is the most important. In many undergraduate music education programs much attention is given to organizing, administering, and supervising instrumental or vocal programs in the secondary school. Few courses are offered for the specific needs of the elementary music specialist.

The elementary music specialist must earn greater recognition and professional status both in elementary education and in music education if some of the hoped for accomplishments are to be achieved.

2. *Continued improvements will be made in the preparation of elementary teachers.* Although the majority of school systems expect or hope that the elementary teacher will accept her responsibility to teach music, inadequate provision for training in music is the norm in her undergraduate preparation. And it is rare for the experienced elementary teacher pursuing a master's degree program to be encouraged to take additional work in music.

The point has already been made in regard to the too common procedure of ignoring music education in the practice teaching experience of prospective elementary teachers. The prospective teacher is asked to prepare well developed plans in language arts, social studies, and mathematics. She is carefully observed and criticized as she teaches the planned lessons. However, if no mention is made of plans for music or no one indicates an interest in observing her teach music, it is understandable why the prospective teacher feels that music must be a matter of inconsequential concern. There is no better way to establish a pattern of *not teaching music* than to allow this to happen during the practice teaching experience. This is a matter that can be and must be rectified.

It seems rather surprising that the elementary music specialist is expected to spend a minimum of four years of intensive training to prepare herself to do a job which the elementary teacher is expected to perform, though with less skill, after having completed as little as one three-hour course in music education. And in some states it is still possible for the elementary major to be certified with no college preparation in music. Institutions of higher learning and, specifically, colleges of education and departments of music must do everything possible to assure a minimum of at least one year in music education for the elementary major. Growth in musicianship, even minimal musicianship, takes time.

However, a good deal of the burden of proof rests squarely with the college music offerings. There is much room for improvement. Courses must be made more functional. In planning college music education courses more attention must be given to the minimum skills the beginning teacher needs in order to do an acceptable job of music teaching. We not only need more preparation, we need better preparation.

Regardless of the size of the college music faculty, at least one person should have the major responsibility for the preparation of elementary teachers and elementary music specialists. The too common practice of "filling in" a staff member's schedule with music education classes regardless of his qualifications to teach them is extremely poor. If the quality of the elementary music education program is to improve, improvements in music education at the college level must also be made.

3. *Consultant relationships will improve.* The three people directly involved in consultant relationships are the consultant, the teacher, and the principal. Before a vital program can be developed, the following conditions must exist:

A. All three must recognize that experiences in music are not only desirable but necessary in the aesthetic growth of children.
B. All three must be willing to work together cooperatively to bring about improved offerings.
C. All three must agree on each one's respective contributions. The elementary teacher must accept her responsibility to teach music as she teaches any subject.

The consultant must accept her responsibility for developing a program of sequential skills and experiences as well as to offer help, guidance, and leadership. The principal must provide encouragement, supervision, and administrative coordination.

Much of the college preparation of the consultant is given over to methods and materials. More attention must be given to consultant relationships. The problem resolves itself to working well with people. The success or failure of the music consultant is largely dependent on effective personal interactions with elementary teachers, a skill too often obtained through "hit and miss" experiences on the job. Much more attention to this phase of her work must be given in undergraduate preparation.

4. *Greater emphasis will be given to in-service education.* Elementary music consultants must do more than they are now doing to provide in-service professional education for elementary teachers. In most situations, the contact of the elementary music consultant with elementary teachers is limited to the twenty or thirty minutes spent in the classroom during the course of her periodic visit. There is little opportunity for the consultant and teacher to react on a person-to-person basis. The consultant may work for several years without really getting to know the teacher either socially or professionally under such conditions.

From our investigation of current practice, we know that in-service work in music education is not widespread. Although the consultant will probably take the initiative for group work, the support of the principal is important. It is easy to understand that an elementary music consultant may feel it presumptuous to push too hard for in-service study if there is resistance. The principal will need to provide the necessary leadership and coordination.

5. *More action research will be undertaken.* Music educators, by and large, have not been research minded either in terms of conducting their own research or in taking advantage of the findings of other research workers. We need to examine the content of our program and we also need to examine carefully the kinds of attitudes we hope to develop as well as the kinds of musical skills and competencies that are required to develop these attitudes.

Research is needed to help us find the answers. Many of our grade level musical goals, for example, are arbitrary. Can we defend them? How much do we know about the developmental abilities and limitations of children? For example, should simple wind instruments be introduced in the third grade or the fourth grade? Does it make any difference? The answer to the question lies not in musical considerations alone but in developmental skills, in readiness, in physical coordination, and in interest maturity.

To what extent are we aware of the work of Carl Orff or Béla Bartók or Zoltán Kodály in the field of elementary music education? How applicable are their principles to our own teaching situations?

How do we go about evaluating musical growth? How do we know that we are extending the musical responsiveness of the boys and girls in our classes?

We need to use the available research to improve our practices. But even more important, music educators must learn the basic principles for conducting research and must participate in meaningful research projects. There is a great need for action research in the field of elementary music education, and more attention must be given to it in the future.

Conclusion

The theory of elementary music education is far in advance of actual practice. We know much more about what we should do than we are doing. Programs have been well developed in innumerable curriculum guides and set forth in any number of basic music series. However, there is a wide disparity in most situations between the program in writing and the program in action. The implementation of a program is a great deal more difficult to bring about than to outline it on paper.

It is sincerely hoped that our thinking about elementary music will not remain static. However, we can make dramatic progress by simply putting into action what has already been outlined in considerable detail. To bring present theory into practice, to further improve the quality of musical experiences, and to give elementary teachers the guidance and help that are necessary, the role of the elementary music consultant will continue to take on increasing importance in the years ahead.

The school is an extension of the society it serves. With the increased attention that is being given to the arts in our contemporary culture, with the tremendous technology that has been developed and will continue to develop to make music readily available to every segment of our society, with the increased leisure available to the American adult, there is no doubt that the expressive arts will play an increasingly important role in the curriculum of the elementary school of the future.

Summary

In this concluding chapter we have considered the following future implications for the direction that elementary music education will take: (1) there is an obvious trend toward a *music-oriented* program, (2) there will be continuing efforts to make music a more integral part of elementary education, and (3) there is a need to understand more clearly the contribution music can make toward personality fulfillment.

There will be a greater rather than a lesser need for specialist help in a program emphasizing musical values and musical learnings. Both teachers and administrators will continue to seek specialist help and parents will continue to expect improved musical experiences for their children in the good elementary school. Some of the predictable trends in elementary music education are: (1) elementary music specialists will achieve improved status within the profession, (2) improvements will continue to be made in the preparation of elementary teachers, (3) consultant relationships will receive greater attention, (4) more emphasis will be placed on in-service education, and (5) more action research will be undertaken.

Questions for Discussion

1. What is meant by a "social-studies-oriented" music series? Investigate several of the available music series and evaluate them in terms of social studies or music emphasis. (The tables of contents will offer helpful clues.)

2. In what ways might a concern for growth and development principles affect the preparation of a curriculum guide in music?

3. Do you feel that more or less specialist help will be required in the elementary school of the future?

4. What kind of help does the administrator want from the elementary music specialist?

5. Can the elementary music specialist be given improved professional status? What are some things she must do to earn improved status?

6. How would you react as an elementary music specialist to a situation where the principal is quite indifferent to the music program? What are some steps that it would be professionally acceptable for you to take?

7. What is meant by the statement, "establishing a pattern of not teaching music during the practice teaching experience"?

8. What would you recommend as a practical, realistic undergraduate program in music education to prepare the elementary teacher to do a creditable job of music teaching?

9. Discuss several action research projects that you think would be helpful to elementary music education.

10. Select one of the following and report on his work in music education: Carl Orff, Béla Bartók, Zoltán Kodály.

Bibliography

Adams, Harold P. and Frank G. Dickey, *Basic Principles of Supervision.* New York: American Book Company, 1953.

American Association of School Administrators, *American School Curriculum.* Washington, D. C.: National Education Association, 1953.

Andrews, Frances M., "Issues and Problems in Music Education," *Music Educators Journal,* Sept.–Oct., 1962.

Andrews, Frances M. and Clara E. Cockerille, *Your School Music Program.* Englewood Cliffs, N. J.: Prentice-Hall, Inc., 1958.

Ayer, Fred C., *Fundamentals of Instructional Supervision.* New York: Harper & Row, Publishers, 1954.

Barr, Avril S., William R. Burton, and Leo J. Bruckner, *Supervision: Democratic Leadership in the Improvement of Learning.* 2nd ed. New York: Appleton-Century-Crofts, 1947.

Bartky, A. John, *Supervision as Human Relations.* Boston: D. C. Heath & Company, 1953.

Benn, Oleta A., "Excellence in Elementary Music Programs," *Music Educators Journal,* Nov.–Dec., 1962.

Bergethon, Bjornar and Eunice Boardman, *Musical Growth in the Elementary School.* New York: Holt, Rinehart, & Winston, Inc., 1963.

Birge, Edward Bailey, *History of Public School Music in the United States.* Bryn Mawr, Pa.: Oliver Ditson Co., 1937.

Britton, Allen P., "Music Education: An American Specialty," *Music Educators Journal,* June–July, 1962.

———, "Music Education in the Nineteen-Sixties," *Music Educators Journal,* June–July, 1961.

Butts, R. Freeman, *A Cultural History of Education.* New York: McGraw-Hill Book Company, 1947.

Colwell, Richard, "Evaluation: Its Use and Significance," *Music Educators Journal,* Feb.–March, 1963.

Cooperative Study of Secondary School Evaluation, *Evaluative Criteria.*

Washington, D. C.: National Study of Secondary School Evaluation, 1960.

Corey, Stephen Maxwell, *Action Research to Improve School Practices*. New York: Bureau of Publications, Teachers College, Columbia University, 1953.

Cremin, Lawrence A., *The American Common School*. New York: Bureau of Publications, Teachers College, Columbia University, 1951.

Crosby, Muriel, *Supervision as Cooperative Action*. New York: Appleton-Century-Crofts, 1957.

Davies, Daniel R. and Fred W. Hosler, *The Challenge of School Board Membership*. New York: Chartwell House, Inc., 1951.

Dewey, John, *Art as Experience*. New York: Minton, Balch and Co., 1934.

————, *The Child and the Curriculum*. Chicago: The University of Chicago Press, 1902.

Educational Policies Commission, *The Central Purpose of American Education*. Washington, D. C.: National Education Association, 1961.

Elsbree, Willard S. and Harold J. McNally, *Elementary School Administration and Supervision*. New York: American Book Company, 1951.

Franseth, Jane, *Supervision as Leadership*. Evanston, Ill.: Harper & Row, Publishers, 1961.

Gaston, E. Thayer, "Aesthetic Experience in Music," *Music Educators Journal,* June–July, 1963.

Hartsell, O. M., *Teaching Music in the Elementary School: Opinion and Comment*. Washington, D. C.: Association for Supervision and Curriculum Development, 1963.

Hermann, Edward J., *The Music Teacher and Public Relations*. Washington, D. C.: The Music Educators National Conference, 1958.

Hood, Marguerite V., "Our Changing School Music Program," *Music Educators Journal,* Feb.–March, 1962.

Howerton, George, "Music As One of the Humanities," *Music Educators Journal,* Sept.–Oct., 1962.

International Society for Music Education, *The Present State of Music Education in the World,* Egon Kraus, ed. Cologne, Germany: The Society, 1960.

Jersild, Arthur T., *Child Psychology*. 5th ed. Englewood Cliffs, N. J.: Prentice-Hall, Inc., 1960.

Lang, Paul Henry, *Music in Western Civilization*. New York: W. W. Norton & Company, Inc., 1941.

Langer, Susanne K., *Feeling and Form*. New York: Charles Scribner's Sons, 1953.

Leonhard, Charles and Robert W. House, *Foundations and Principles of Music Education*. New York: McGraw-Hill Book Company, 1959.

McNerney, Chester T., *Educational Supervision*. New York: McGraw-Hill Book Company, 1951.

Miel, Alice, *Changing the Curriculum, A Social Process*. New York: Appleton-Century-Crofts, 1946.

Mursell, James L., *Education for Musical Growth*. Boston: Ginn & Company, 1948.

———, *Music and the Classroom Teacher*. Morristown, N. J.: Silver Burdett Co., 1951.

———, *Music Education Principles and Programs*. Morristown, N. J.: Silver Burdett Co., 1956.

Music Educators National Conference, *Music Supervision and Administration in the Schools*. Washington, D. C.: The Conference, 1949.

———, *The Study of Music: An Academic Discipline*. Washington, D. C.: The Conference, 1963.

Myers, Louise Kifer, *Teaching Children Music in the Elementary School*. 3rd ed. Englewood Cliffs, N. J.: Prentice-Hall, Inc., 1961.

National Education Association, *Deciding What to Teach*. Washington, D. C.: The Association, 1963.

———, *Education in a Changing Society*. Washington, D. C.: The Association, 1963.

———, *Music and Art in the Public Schools*. Washington, D. C.: Research Division of the Association, 1963.

National Society for the Study of Education, *Basic Concepts in Music Education*. Fifty-seventh Yearbook, Part I, Nelson B. Henry, ed. Chicago: The Society, 1958.

Nye, Robert E., *Music for Elementary School Children*. New York, N. Y.: The Center for Applied Research in Education, Inc., 1963.

Nye, Robert E. and Vernice T. Nye, *Music in the Elementary School*. 2nd ed. Englewood Cliffs, N. J.: Prentice-Hall, Inc., 1964.

Orff, Carl and Gunild Keetman, *Music for Children*. Part I, Pentatonic, trans. Doreen Hall and Arnold Walter. New York: Associated Music Publishers, Inc., 1955.

Pierce, Anne E., *Teaching Music in the Elementary School*. New York: Holt, Rinehart & Winston, Inc., 1959.

Pitts, Lilla Belle, *Music Curriculum in a Changing World*. New York: Silver Burdett Co., 1944.

Prescott, Daniel A., *The Child in the Educative Process*. New York: McGraw-Hill Book Company, 1957.

Reeder, Edwin H., *Supervision in the Elementary School*. Boston: Houghton Mifflin Company, 1953.

Replogle, V. L., "What Help Do Teachers Want?" *Educational Leadership*, April, 1950.

Richards, Mary Helen, *Threshold to Music*. San Francisco: Fearon Publishers, 1964.

Sachs, Curt, *Our Musical Heritage*. 2nd ed. Englewood Cliffs, N. J.: Prentice-Hall, Inc., 1955.

Snyder, Alice M., *Creating Music with Children*. New York: Mills Music, Inc., 1957.

Snyder, Keith D., *School Music Administration and Supervision*. Boston: Allyn and Bacon, Inc., 1959.

Southern Association's Cooperative Study in Elementary Education, *Evaluating the Elementary School*. Atlanta, Georgia: Southern Association Commission on Research and Service, 1951.

Swanson, Bessie R., *Music in the Education of Children*. Belmont, Calif.: Wadsworth Publishing Co., 1961.

Swearingen, Mildred E., *Supervision of Instruction*. Boston: Allyn and Bacon, Inc., 1962.

Tipton, Gladys, "The Changing Emphasis in Music Materials," *The Instructor*, March, 1964.

U. S. Department of Health, Education, and Welfare, Office of Education, "Role of the Special Teacher," *School Life*, March, 1957.

————, *Music in Our Schools: A Search for Improvement*. Washington, D. C.: Office of Education, 1964.

Wiles, Kimball, *Supervision for Better Schools*. 2nd ed. Englewood Cliffs, N. J.: Prentice-Hall, Inc., 1955.

Index

A

Accent, 76–77
Accreditation, 139
Achievement tests, musical, 144
Action research:
  consultant participation, 107
  need for, 192
  renewed emphasis, 186
Administration:
  complementary to supervision, 134
  consultant's responsibility, 65
  consultant's skill in, 147
  coordinating, 138
  defined, 134
  evaluating, 138
  expectation for music teaching, 184
  interpreting, 139
  organizing, 138
  planning, 137
  supervisor of music, 134
  top-level administrators, 137
Adult level music, 93
Aesthetic experiences:
  in adult life, 190
  concern for, 14
  current emphasis, 173
  essentials, 14
Affective processes, 26
Aiken, Charles, 165
Aims of:
  education, 13
  elementary music education, 3, 14–16
  elementary music supervision, 8, 40–44
  supervision, 38
American Association of School Administrators, 169
Andrews, Frances M., 10
"Answer" phrases, 77
Approach, cooperative:
  administrative organization, 138
  common practice, 182
  consultant, 6–7

Approach, cooperative (cont.)
  correlation, 7
  current status, 173
  defined, 6
  described, 6–8
  elementary teacher, 6–7
  impediments, 9
  principal, 6
  promising practice, 6
  shared responsibilities (diagram), 7
Approaches:
  current, 3, 4
  to music teaching, 3
  to musical learning, 71, 98
Aptitude tests, musical, 144
Art:
  attainments, 82
  in everyday life, 189
  meeting of specialists, 53
  need for specialist help, 188
  "new" subject, 50
  supervisor, 168
Assembly singing, 151–152
Atlantic City, 169
Attention span, 32
Attitude:
  of elementary teachers, 53, 112–113
  expressed concern, 179
  of specialist, 53
  of students, 152, 192
  variations within faculty, 113
Audio-visual aids, 115
Authoritative approach, 50
Autoharp:
  consultant visit, 51
  demonstrations, 128
  selecting chords, 89
Ayer, Fred C., 169, 189

B

Bands, 92, 168
Bartók, Béla, 192

199

Newspaper publicity, 69
Nineteenth century, 163–166, 172
Nine-year-old child, 31, 89
Normal schools, 166
Notebook, consultant's, 100–102
Number of classroom visits daily:
  author's recommendation, 183
  current practice, 176
  recommended practice, 176
Number of teachers served:
  author's recommendation, 183
  current practice, 176
  expressed concern, 179
  recommended practice, 176
Nye, Robert E. and Vernice T. Nye, 174

O

Observation:
  by general supervisor, 39, 50
  by music consultant, 50
  by parents, 45
  by supervisor of music, 133
Official leader, 38
On-call requests, 105
On-call schedule, 124
On-call visits, 53–54 (*see also* Visits)
Orchestra, early development in schools, 166, 168
Orchestral instruments, 88, 90, 93
Orff, Carl, 192
Organization:
  administrative process, 138
  continuity in, 153
  evaluative criteria, 153–154
  of program, 43, 153
Ostinato, 76, 87

P

Palace schools, 160–161
Parents:
  in evaluation, 150
  expect specialist help, 189
  expectations of program, 139–140
  interest in program, 44
Part songs, 90
Participation by teacher during consultant's visit, 52, 117, 136, 148
Patrons, 44–45
Peer approval, 92
Peer relationships:
  of consultant, 40
  of students, 85, 88
  of supervisor of music, 132–133
Peer-group processes, 26

Pentatonic melodies, 76
Percussion classes, beginning, 152
Percussive instruments, 42
Performance, public, 44, 126, 128
Personality fulfillment, 188
Personnel director, 137
Pestalozzi, Johann Heinrich, 163–164
Pestalozzian principles, 163–164
Physical education:
  attainments expected, 82
  meeting of specialists, 53
  "new" subject, 50, 165
  specialist help, 188
  supervisor, 168
Physical processes, 25
Piano class, 56–57, 113
Piano students, 114
Pianos in elementary schools, 128
Pierce, Charles, 167
Pitch, 74
Pitts, Lilla Belle, 14, 167
Pittsburgh, 164
Planning:
  administrative process, 137
  annual, 97–98:
    flexibility, 98
    goals, 97
    typical plan, 97
    written objectives, 98
  beginning-middle-end organization, 101
  a classroom visit, 101
  consultant's work, 96–97
  dangers in improvising, 102
  departure from plan, 102
  involving others, 97
  long-range, 96
  monthly, 97–100:
    flexibility, 98
    musical learnings as topics, 99
    school calendar, 100
    suggested topics, 98–100
    typical plan, 99
  by music consultant, 116
  repeating a lesson, 102
  weekly, 100–104:
    introduction - presentation - conclusion, 102
    plans, 103–104
    typical example, 100
Plato, 160, 173
Playing instruments:
  approach to musical learning, 72
  fifth-grade goals, 92
  first-grade goals, 86
  fourth-grade goals, 90
  goals for all levels, 84
  second-grade goals, 87
  select instruments to match mood, 87
  sixth-grade goals, 93